JOHN F. KENNEDY

PRESIDENTIAL ✦ LEADERS

JOHN F. KENNEDY

CATHERINE CORLEY ANDERSON

LERNER PUBLICATIONS COMPANY/MINNEAPOLIS

Lerner Publications Company
A division of Lerner Publishing Group
241 First Avenue North
Minneapolis, MN 55401 U.S.A.

Website address: www.lernerbooks.com

Library of Congress Cataloging-in-Publication Data

Anderson, Catherine Corley.
    John F. Kennedy / by Catherine Corley Anderson.
        p.   cm. — (Presidential leaders)
    Summary: A biography of the dynamic leader who served as the thirty-fifth president of the United States until his assassination in 1963.
    Includes bibliographical references and index.
    ISBN: 0–8225–0812–5 (lib. bdg. : alk. paper)
    1. Kennedy, John F. (John Fitzgerald), 1917–1963—Juvenile literature. 2. Presidents— United States—Biography—Juvenile literature. [1. Kennedy, John F. (John Fitzgerald), 1917–1963. 2. Presidents.] I. Title. II. Series.
    E842.Z9A628   2004
    973.922'092—dc22   2003016545

Manufactured in the United States of America
1 2 3 4 5 6 – JR – 09 08 07 06 05 04

CONTENTS

———— ✧ ————

Though his time in office was short, President Kennedy earned the love and respect of many people in the United States and outside the country.

CHAPTER ONE

GROWING UP RICH

*"For of those to whom much is given,
much is required."*
—Luke 12:48, a Kennedy family philosophy

The night of August 1, 1943, was dark and eerie as the PT
109, an eighty-foot plywood U.S. patrol torpedo boat, crept
through the shadows of the tropical waters of the Pacific
Ocean. Exotic birds screamed while the men in the crew
remained silent on deck, peering into the darkness. The
United States was in the midst of World War II
(1939–1945). Suddenly, a Japanese enemy destroyer slammed
into PT 109, slicing it in two. Two sailors were killed.
Lieutenant John Fitzgerald Kennedy, the boat's commander,
was hurled against the wall of the cockpit, almost breaking
his back. Flames engulfed the back half of the boat.

Kennedy ordered his crew into the water, then swam out
to search for survivors. At dawn, carrying a badly burned
crew member on his own injured back, Kennedy led the men

in search of safety. After swimming for eight hours, he and his men reached an island. The rest of the crew followed. All eleven survivors were eventually rescued, due in large part to Kennedy's courage and intelligence. The same traits of compassion, courage under pressure, endurance, and a cool, analytical mind would later serve him well during his presidency.

EARLY YEARS

John Fitzgerald Kennedy was born on May 29, 1917, in a big frame house in Brookline, Massachusetts, a suburb of Boston. As a child, Jack, as John soon was called, had several childhood diseases. Perhaps this was why he was small for his age. His older brother, Joe, was much bigger and stronger. Joe took it upon himself to be Jack's coach and protector.

Jack admired his big brother, but it bothered him sometimes to have Joe always telling him what to do. Jack was never as good as Joe in sports and other pursuits, but he tried awfully hard.

Life in the Kennedy household was full of fun and activity. The boys soon had younger sisters. Rosemary was born in 1918, Kathleen came a little more than a year later, and Eunice followed in 1921. In the winter, their father, Joe Kennedy Sr., a very successful businessman, took his children for rides on a homemade sled. In the summer, Grandpa Fitzgerald took them to watch the Boston Red Sox, his favorite baseball team. Rose Kennedy, their mother, often planned family trips to historic places around Boston.

Both parents impressed on their children that the United States had been good to the Kennedys. Whatever benefits the family received *from* the country, they were told, must be returned by performing some service *for* the country.

In 1926 the family moved to Riverdale, New York. Jack spent his grade-school days at Riverdale Country Day School. He was still small and slight for his age. His sixth-grade teacher, Irene Guiney, said he was chiefly noted for his sense of humor and for his desire to excel—mostly in sports. He liked history and English, but he was a very poor speller and not very good in science or math.

At thirteen Jack went away to school for the first time. He attended Canterbury School in New Milford, Connecticut. Jack was pretty homesick the first month. He wrote home to ask for golf balls, a "puff quilt" (his description of a down-filled comforter), and chocolate cream pie. He also asked for thirty-five cents more a week in his allowance to pay his Boy Scout dues, and "to pay my way around."

———————————————— ✧ ————————————————

The Kennedy family, photographed in 1932, from left to right: Bobby, Jack, Eunice, Jean, Joe Sr., Rose, Pat, Kathleen, Joe Jr., and Rosemary

The family had grown to include Patricia, Bobby, Jean, and Edward, who was called Ted or Teddy. Rose Kennedy had servants to help with the housework and her busy, noisy family. Joe Kennedy Sr. bought other homes in West Palm Beach, Florida, and Hyannis Port, Massachusetts.

Jack acquired his love for the sea and learned how to handle small boats at Hyannis Port. He named his first sailboat *Victura,* which meant something about winning, he said. This was in keeping with the Kennedy code, instilled in the children by their father. They were taught that one must always try to be first, to be the best.

At Easter, in 1931, Jack had an attack of appendicitis and was rushed to the hospital. He couldn't finish the spring term at Canterbury. The next fall he enrolled at Choate Preparatory in Wallingford, Connecticut. His older brother, Joe, had

already been there for a year. Joe was on the football, baseball, and hockey teams, and he was very good in his studies.

Jack quickly formed his own circle of friends. Lemoyne (Lem) Billings and Ralph (Rip) Horton were his buddies. With half a

We're puttin' on our top hat,
Tyin' up our white tie,
Brushin' off our tails,
In order to
Wish you

A Merry Christmas

Rip.   Leem.   Ken.

_____ ✧

This Christmas card was sent by Jack (right) *and his roommates Lem Billings* (center) *and Rip Horton* (left).

dozen other boys, they started a club called the "Muckers." The members often got into trouble. Although students were not allowed to leave the school grounds without permission, one night the Muckers sneaked out to the local ice cream parlor after hours. On their way back to their rooms, they ran smack into the headmaster.

The boys were in danger of being expelled, and their parents were notified. When his father arrived at the school, Jack confessed his part in the escapade. He promised his father he would put more effort into his studies. All the boys were given a second chance.

Jack was eighteen when he graduated from Choate in 1934. He had grown tall, lanky, and good-looking, but he still looked much younger than this age. He often wished he were as handsome and polished as his brother Joe.

A LOOK AT EUROPE

Jack had been promised a trip to London as a graduation gift. His father wanted him to attend a summer session at the London School of Economics, but Jack protested. He thought the trip was to be a holiday. He had heard that Professor Harold Laski, who ran the school, was a Communist.

Mr. Kennedy said that he didn't expect Jack to agree with the professor's beliefs but that it was a good idea to learn other points of view besides his own. Jack didn't get much chance to put his view into practice. He had hardly started class when he became ill. He felt weak, and his skin turned yellow. A doctor told him he had jaundice and would have to go to the hospital.

As soon as he was allowed to travel, Jack left for Hyannis Port. He spent the rest of the summer trying to recover. He wasn't entirely well when he started school at Princeton University, several weeks late, in the fall of 1935.

Around Christmas the jaundice recurred, and Jack had to drop out of school. His doctor prescribed rest in a warm climate. Jack went to Arizona, soaked up the sun, and read all the books he could lay his hands on. Before the next school year began, he told his father he wanted to go to Harvard University instead of Princeton.

These were exciting times at school and around the world. On campuses, young people took a keen interest in politics, social changes, and events in Europe. The United States was pulling out of the Great Depression, which had gripped the country in the 1930s. The Depression had begun in 1929 with the collapse of the stock market and the widespread failure of banks and businesses. Breadlines and soup kitchens—where hungry people stood in line for handouts of food—had become a common sight. One out of four workers was unemployed.

Joe Kennedy Sr.'s insight and shrewd maneuvers had saved him from financial disaster. He bought stocks at very low prices and held them until their value increased. Then, at just the right moment, he sold them and made a large profit.

While in college, Jack first became aware of the vast social and economic differences in the United States. The fellows at school talked about such things, and Jack, a rich man's son, came in for some good-natured kidding. But Jack cared about poor people and wondered what he could do to help them.

Jack's father had supported Franklin Delano Roosevelt when he ran for president in 1932. Roosevelt won the

election. When he became president, Roosevelt started many
programs to help the unemployed and to get the economy
back to normal. In an effort to
prevent the careless and dishon-
est business practices that con-
tributed to the collapse of the
economy in 1929, Congress cre-
ated the Securities and Exchange
Commission to set up regulations for the stock market. In
return for Kennedy's support
during the presidential campaign,
Roosevelt appointed him chair-
person of the new commission.

Franklin Delano Roosevelt

———————— ✧ ————————

President Roosevelt was also watching events in Europe.
In 1937 President Roosevelt appointed Joseph Kennedy to
be the U.S. ambassador to Great Britain. It was an important position, and the appointment made Mr. Kennedy
very happy. Joe Jr. and Jack stayed at Harvard, but the rest
of the family moved to Great Britain. The British were
charmed by the handsome Kennedys, and the Kennedys
enjoyed living in London.

Meanwhile, Europe was teetering on the edge of war.
Ambassador Kennedy kept President Roosevelt informed
about events taking place. In September 1938, Prime
Minister Neville Chamberlain of Great Britain met with the
German dictator, Adolf Hitler, in Munich, Germany. In an
attempt to stop Hitler's territorial expansion and avoid war,
Chamberlain agreed to allow the Germans to take over a

Adolf Hitler (right) *broke his promise to Neville Chamberlain* (left)
that Czechoslovakia would be Germany's last invasion. Soon after,
most of Europe was propelled into World War II.

part of Czechoslovakia. In return, Hitler promised that it
would be his last territorial claim. Hitler had already sent
Nazi troops into the Rhineland, a region of Germany along
the Rhine River, and Austria. (According to the Treaty of
Versailles, which officially ended World War I in 1919, the
Rhineland was to remain free of German troops.)

Within a few months, however, Hitler broke his
promise and took control of all of Czechoslovakia. Soon
afterward he attacked Poland. Since Great Britain and
France had pledged to defend Poland, they declared war on
Germany. On September 1, 1939, World War II began.
Ambassador Kennedy advised Roosevelt that the United
States should not become involved in what he considered a
European war.

CHAPTER TWO

IS IT OUR WAR?

"For without belittling [undervaluing]
*the courage with which men have died,
we should not forget those acts of courage
with which men . . . have* lived.*"*

Profiles in Courage, John F. Kennedy

Jack had been traveling in Europe during the spring and
summer of 1939. He had obtained permission from
Harvard to spend the spring term in Europe as part of his
work for his major in political science. After visiting his
family and talking to his father in London, Jack went on
an unofficial journey of observation for the ambassador. He
spent several months in Paris, then traveled to Poland,
Latvia, the Soviet Union, Turkey, Palestine, the Balkans,
and Belgium. Everywhere he went, he talked to people on
the street as well as to officials at the various embassies.

Ambassador Kennedy continued to speak out against
U.S. involvement in what he considered European politics—

thus losing his popularity with the British, who wanted U.S. support. He thought Great Britain and France didn't stand a chance against the well-trained and well-equipped Nazi German army.

On September 3, 1939, Ambassador Kennedy was awakened by a telephone call in the middle of the night. He was told that an unarmed British passenger ship, the *Athenia*, had been torpedoed by a German submarine. Many Americans—310—had been aboard.

The ambassador woke Jack, who had been sleeping in the next room, and told him what had happened. Survivors were being taken to Glasgow, Scotland. He wanted Jack to leave at once for Glasgow to help the survivors and to find out exactly what had occurred. It was a big job for a twenty-two-year-old.

———————————— ✧ ————————————

Survivors of the Athenia *tragedy disembark from the* Knute Nelson, *the Norwegian tanker that rescued them.*

When Jack reached Glasgow, he found a scene of tragedy, courage, and indignation. He assured U.S. passengers that space would be found for them on other ships. Jack was just as angry as they were about the attack on an unarmed passenger ship.

As the war progressed, the ambassador became concerned about protecting his family. To ensure their safety, he sent his family home to the United States, but he stayed at his post in London.

A NEW SENSE OF PURPOSE

That fall Jack returned to Harvard a much more mature and thoughtful young man. He began to study with real purpose for the first time in his life. Professor Arthur N. Holcombe, who taught political science, wrote of Jack's scholarship:

> *He had a genuine and deep interest in ideas, and courses which presented ideas so as to bring out their practical importance in life. . . . When he had work to do which interested him, he threw all of his great energy and fine intelligence into it, producing results of superior quality.*

Jack missed the earlier, carefree times he'd had with his friends, and he missed playing football. As a Harvard freshman, he had been first-string end on the freshman squad. He and his friend Torb McDonald had practiced passing and receiving until they were so good that the coach had used them as the opposing offense in practice games against the varsity team. In one of the practice games against the bigger, stronger varsity team, Jack received an injury to his back that caused him much suffering for the rest of his life.

However, Jack realized that other things were more important than sports. It was time to write his senior thesis. Jack had been thinking about Great Britain, Hitler, and the apathy—the lack of concern—on the part of the British people before the war. After much studying, writing, and rewriting, he finished his thesis, "Appeasement at Munich." It was outstanding in its analysis of Europe's and Great Britain's crisis. Two of Jack's professors thought it was good enough to be published.

In June 1940, Jack graduated cum laude (with praise or distinction) from Harvard. His thesis earned a magna cum laude (great praise). Mr. Kennedy could not leave his post in London, but Rose Kennedy and all Jack's sisters went to Boston for the festivities of commencement week.

After graduation, Jack Kennedy began to send his thesis to

publishers, and it was accepted on the second try. Wilfred Funk published it under the title *Why England Slept*. It became a best-seller. Kennedy became a literary sensation.

✧ ————————

Kennedy's first book, based on his senior thesis, was a hit with critics and quickly became a best-seller.

During the summer of 1940 in Hyannis Port, the games of touch football and tennis, the swimming and sailing went on at a furious pace. Family discussions at Hyannis Port centered on the part the United States would or should play in World War II. It was the same topic people were talking about all over the land.

Only Rosemary stood outside the charmed circle. It had gradually become apparent to the Kennedys that Rosemary was not like the rest of the family. Rosemary was developmentally disabled. She had wild, violent moods, and she was retreating into a world of her own. Finally, she was confined to a care center in Wisconsin.

THE WAR SPREADS

In Europe the Nazi armies had overtaken the Netherlands, Denmark, and Romania. France had fallen. Only the poorly armed British army stood in the way of a German victory over all of Europe. The United States was sending supplies and war materials, but it had not yet declared war.

Because of his opposition to the war, Joseph Kennedy's popularity continued to decrease in Britain and in many circles in the United States. In October 1940, he resigned his post as ambassador and returned to the United States.

Both Jack Kennedy and his brother Joe wanted to volunteer in the armed services. In the spring, Joe had been accepted as a naval air cadet. Both the army and the navy rejected Jack because of his back trouble and his history of illness. But he used his fighting spirit to overcome those obstacles. He bought special gym equipment and barbells and worked out every day. Each morning he took a cross-country run. He was determined to build up his weak back muscles.

Kennedy had been around water and small boats most of his life. He felt sure that the navy could use his experience. In September he tried again. This time he made it, but much to his disgust, he was assigned to a desk job in Washington. That wasn't what Kennedy wanted at all. He applied for a transfer.

On December 7, 1941, an act occurred that finally brought the United States into World War II. The Japanese air force carried out a surprise attack on the U.S. naval fleet at Pearl Harbor, Hawaii. Most of the fleet was destroyed, and thousands were killed or wounded. The next day, the United States formally declared war on Japan. On December 11, Germany and Italy declared war on the United States.

Six months later, Kennedy was sent to the Naval Officers Training School at Northwestern University in Evanston, Illinois. Later he was assigned to the Motor Torpedo Boat Center at Melville, Rhode Island.

One day on the grounds of the center, Kennedy noticed a game of touch football. It was a free period for Kennedy, so he strolled over and asked if he could get in the game. The young man who was calling the plays, Paul Fay, thought Kennedy was a high school kid. He was dressed in an inside-out Harvard sweater, baggy trousers, and sneakers.

The "kid" turned out to be a fast and furious player, Fay said later. Much to Fay's embarrassment, the tall, thin young man also turned out to be Fay's instructor in small boat handling!

CHAPTER THREE

THIS IS HOW IT FEELS

*"Previously, I had become somewhat cynical
about the American as a fighting man. I had
seen too much bellyaching and laying off. But
with the chips down—all that faded away."*
—John F. Kennedy, in a letter to his parents, 1943

The PT (patrol torpedo) boat was a fast, light, eighty-foot-long motorboat made of plywood. It had four torpedo tubes and carried four fifty-caliber machine guns and an antiaircraft gun. The boat moved easily in and out of the twisting waterways around the small islands that make up the Solomon Islands in the South Pacific. Because of its light construction, a PT boat gave little protection to its crew. PT crews depended on the boat's speed of forty knots per hour and its ability to maneuver to escape harm from enemy boats.

On the island of Tulagi in late April 1943, Lieutenant John F. Kennedy was put in command of PT 109, a dirty, weather-beaten veteran of many battles. Kennedy was dismayed at his first sight of PT 109. He immediately ordered that the boat be put into dry dock for cleaning and repairs.

READY FOR DUTY

One holdover from the former crew was still there: Leonard Thom, former football star at Ohio State. Kennedy made Ensign Thom his executive officer, and together they chose a crew. The PT crew liked Kennedy because he treated them fairly and worked harder than any of them. They scraped, sanded, and painted the hull, engine room, and lower quarters of PT 109. With the engine cleaned and oiled, and with a coat of fresh, forest green paint, PT 109 was ready for duty.

U.S. forces were working a slow passage through the Solomon Sea toward Rabaul, a Japanese stronghold. On the

———————————— ✧ ————————————

Kennedy (far right) poses with his crew aboard PT 109. Back row, left to right: Allan Webb, Leon Drawdy, Edgar E. Mauer, Edmund Drewditch, John McGuire. Front row, left to right: Charles "Bucky" Harris, Maurice Kowal, Andrew Kirksey, and Leonard Thom.

night of August 1, 1943, word came that the "Tokyo Express," Japanese ships that made periodic raids through the waters of the Solomons, was coming again. A fleet of fifteen PT boats was sent out to intercept the Japanese.

Something was eerie about those night patrols down shadowy streams overhung with tropical growth. The only sounds were the screams of exotic tropical birds, the occasional splash of a crocodile, and the hushed drone of the engine. The water was luminous, and the crews couldn't be sure if a dark shape was an enemy ship, a trick of light or shadow, or another PT boat.

To reduce noise, PT 109 crept along on one engine. Lieutenant Kennedy peered into the darkness. On the foredeck, Engineer John Maguire said his prayers. Ensign George "Barney" Ross stood over a 37-millimeter gun the crew had lashed to the foredeck. Ross had been a last-minute volunteer to the crew. Nineteen-year-old Harold Marney, newest member of the crew, was in the forward gun turret. Suddenly, he shouted, "Ship at two o'clock!"

A Japanese destroyer, the *Amagiri,* was almost on top of them. Kennedy ordered Maguire, "Sound general quarters!" It was too late. There was no time to launch a torpedo or to change course. The *Amagiri's* steel hull caused a grinding crunch as it tore into the plywood frame of PT 109. Marny was crushed to death. Kennedy was hurled against the wall of the cockpit so hard it almost broke his back. His first thought, he related afterward, was "So this is how it feels to die."

The *Amagiri* had cut PT 109 in two. The stern, or back half of the boat, was engulfed in flames. The bow section, the front, was still afloat. Because he was afraid that fire would break out in the bow, Kennedy ordered everyone into the water. Ross and Maguire were with him in the bow. Kennedy swam out to search for survivors. The raging flames against the black sky were almost blinding. Even the water was on fire from spilled gasoline.

It took almost superhuman effort to get the men, exhausted and injured, back onto the still-afloat bow. Pat McMahon had been seriously burned. Kennedy called roll and found everyone present except Marney and Kirksey. They had been killed in the crash.

Until dawn the eleven survivors huddled in the bow and tried to decide what to do. In the dark, they didn't know their exact location, and many of the small islands on both sides of Blackett Strait were inhabited by the Japanese. As the shadows lifted, the men were in danger of being seen by the enemy.

IN SEARCH OF AN ISLAND

Then what was left of PT 109 overturned, pitching them all into the water. Fortunately, Kennedy had taken inventory of what supplies they had left. Besides a blinker light, they had a ship's lantern, several life jackets, a Thompson submachine gun, some small arms, and three knives. They would have to swim to an island, but McMahon had third-degree burns over half his body and couldn't possibly make it alone. Kennedy and his crew faced the worst of their ordeal.

Kennedy cut one end of McMahon's life jacket strap. Kennedy put the loose end of the strap into his mouth and clamped down hard with his teeth. Slipping under McMahon, he began to swim while towing McMahon on his back. He said nothing about his own back injury. The others tied what supplies they had to a plank of wood. They used the wooden plank for support in the water as they swam.

Kennedy's strong, steady strokes soon took him and McMahon out of sight of the others. Time began to blur. Kennedy had no idea he had been in the water for eight hours. Then he caught sight of an island. He could tell from its size and shape that it was Plum Pudding Island. The tall casuarina trees would hide them from Japanese planes.

Trying to ignore the pain in his back, Kennedy reached the rocky shore. The two men fell, exhausted, under some bushes and rested. At last Kennedy sat up and looked out across the water. He was overjoyed to see the plank, with nine bobbing heads alongside, nearing the shore. They, too, fell headlong on the shore and rested or slept. When they couldn't find any edible plants or water, Kennedy realized they couldn't stay there long.

After sundown Kennedy swam out into Ferguson Passage. He hoped to be able to hail a patrolling PT boat. He hadn't had anything to eat or drink for eighteen hours. His back was burning with pain. He wore shoes that he had salvaged from the wreck and carried a revolver tied around his neck. After treading water for hours, Kennedy was forced to admit that no patrol boats were coming. Eventually, he swam back to Plum Pudding Island.

Two days later, the entire crew swam to Olasana, another island closer to Ferguson Passage. Kennedy again towed McMahon. On Olasana they found coconut palm trees. They smashed coconuts on the coral rocks and drank the milk eagerly. But after three days of no food or drink, they got sick. Kennedy tried to keep up the spirits of the men, but they all knew their situation was dangerous.

Kennedy and Ross set off for the island of Naru the next day. When they landed on its sandy shore, they found a supply of rainwater, a large wooden box of hard candy, and a canoe. The supplies had been left there by native scouts.

The canoe that Kennedy and Ross had found was just big enough for one person, plus the supplies. Ross stayed on Naru while Jack started back to Olasana.

When Kennedy arrived at Olasana, a cheerful fire was burning on the shore. Two Melanesian boys had arrived before him and had shared some native food with the happy crew. Leonard Thom, the big, blond ex-football star, had waded out into the water and convinced the canoeists that the crew was friendly.

Kennedy couldn't stay to celebrate with them. He had to hurry back to Naru where he had left Ross. The Melanesians took him back in their canoe. They covered Kennedy with leaves to hide him in case they were seen by the Japanese. Finally, a huge wave picked them up and deposited them on the shore of Naru.

Kennedy picked up a coconut, scraped off some of the shell, and carved a message. It said:

NARU ISL./
NATIVE KNOWS POSIT [position]
HE CAN PILOT/11 ALIVE/
NEED SMALL BOAT
KENNEDY

He pointed to Rendova Peak, which could be seen all over the area, and said, "Rendova." The Melanesians seemed to understand.

Unknown to Kennedy, the Melanesians were scouts, working for Lieutenant Reginald Evans, an Australian coast

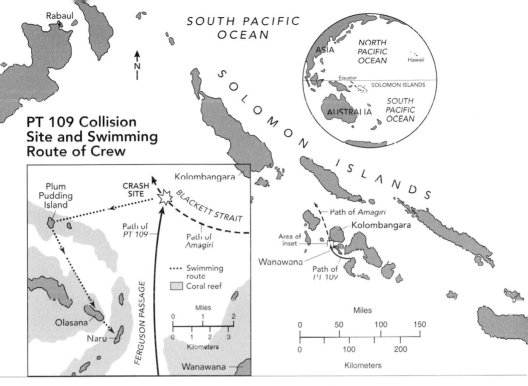

Kennedy and his PT 109 crew spent several days swimming among the Solomon Islands in the South Pacific before they were rescued.

---

watcher. (A network of coast watchers hidden in the Solomon Islands watched for enemy ships and planes and reported their positions to friendly ships in the area.) The scouts took the message to Evans. Evans then sent another scout in a canoe with food, water, and a message for Kennedy. Through Evans a plan was set up, and a PT boat was sent to the rescue.

Kennedy refused home leave in the United States and was given another boat, PT 59. Some of his old crew volunteered to serve with him. They continued the strenuous work of patrolling. Twice they took part in rescues of marine patrols.

THE AFTERMATH

Kennedy was in constant pain from his back injury. Eventually, he contracted malaria, became very ill, and lost twenty-five pounds. Even he had to admit that he was no longer fit for duty. He was forced to give up his command and was sent home to Chelsea Naval Hospital near Hyannis Port.

Kennedy was allowed to leave the hospital on weekends to spend time with the family at Hyannis Port. It seemed almost like old times, except that Joe, Kathleen (whom he always called "Kick"), and Rosemary weren't there. Young Joe Kennedy was flying dangerous missions for the Allies along the coast of Belgium and feeling somewhat jealous of his younger brother's accomplishments and celebrity. Against the wishes of her Catholic parents, Kathleen had married an English officer, a Protestant, whose family was a member of the British aristocracy, or upper class.

Kennedy's back didn't get any better, and he was weak and tired. Finally, he decided to follow his doctors' advice, and he had an operation on his spine in the summer of 1944. The operation didn't go well, and Jack was flat on his back in a hospital bed when he received the worst blow of all. Joseph P. Kennedy Jr. had been killed in action. Joe's accident happened on August 12, 1944, a little more than a year after the PT 109 collision.

Kennedy fought his grief and ill health, but only a month later, Kathleen's husband was killed in France. Kathleen was home with the family in Hyannis Port when she got the news. They all drew closer together in their sorrow.

Kennedy had always thought of his brother Bobby as a freckle-faced kid, but Bobby was growing up. After Joe's death, Bobby resigned from the officers' training program at Harvard and asked for service on the new destroyer USS *Joseph P. Kennedy,* named after his dead brother. His request was granted.

MILITARY HERO

As a result of his PT 109 ordeal, Kennedy received the Purple Heart, the Navy and Marine Corps Medal, and a citation in 1944 from Admiral W. F. Halsey, commander of U.S. forces in the South Pacific. The citation read, in part:

> *For heroism in the rescue of three men following the ramming and sinking of his motor torpedo boat . . . on the night of August 1–2, 1943. Lieutenant KENNEDY, Captain of the boat, directed the rescue of the crew and personally rescued three men. . . . His courage, endurance and excellent leadership contributed to the saving of several lives and was in keeping with the highest traditions of the United States Naval Service.*

---◇---

Captain F. L. Conklin presents the Navy and Marine Corps Medal to Kennedy at the Chelsea Naval Hospital in Massachusetts in 1944.

CHAPTER FOUR

HITTING THE CAMPAIGN TRAIL

"A man does what he must . . . in spite of
obstacles and dangers and pressures—and that
is the basis of all human morality."
—*Profiles in Courage*, John F. Kennedy

In November 1944, Franklin Delano Roosevelt was elected president for a fourth term. One of Roosevelt's favorite projects was the establishment of the United Nations, an organization dedicated to world peace and the betterment of humanity. Just two weeks before the United Nations Conference was to meet, President Roosevelt died suddenly. Vice President Harry S. Truman became president.

The United Nations was to hold its first official meeting in San Francisco, California, in April 1945. The Hearst newspapers, a chain of newspapers owned by William Randolph Hearst, needed a correspondent with foreign experience to report on the meeting. Kennedy was offered the job, and he was glad to accept.

Kennedy wrote this article about the UN Conference in San Francisco for the New York Journal American.

Serviceman's View of Conference

Soviet Diplomacy Gets 50-50 Break

(Lt. John F. Kennedy, recently retired PT Boat hero of the South Pacific and son of Former Ambassador Joseph P. Kennedy, is covering the San Francisco United Nations Conference from a serviceman's point of view for the N. Y. Journal-American. Before the war he authored the best seller "Why England Slept.")

By JOHN F. KENNEDY
Special to the N. Y. Journal-American

SAN FRANCISCO, May 3.—The word is out more or less officially that Molotov is about to pick up his marbles and go home. He'll leave his delegation here to carry out the important detailed work. This news comes as no surprise because as the spotlight turns toward Europe and the war's ending—not only Molotov but many of the reporters are getting ready to head east.

Diplomacy might be said to be on the second day of the conference when a reporter asked Mr. Molotov whether he was in favor of admitting Argentina to the United Nations Conference.

Kennedy went to San Francisco with a feeling that perhaps this was something important. He wanted to be where the action was. He watched the proceedings with a keen eye. Kennedy informed his readers that many delegates were extremely suspicious of the delegates from the Soviet Union. Others thought that in "their own strange and inexplicable way they really want peace."

Kennedy was finished with college and with his military service, but he was still feeling his way in a quickly changing world. Old attitudes and ideas were giving way to new ones. New, independent nations were emerging in Africa and Asia. The United States and the Soviet Union—anticipating the end of World War II—were engaged in a struggle for power in postwar Europe. World events were exciting, and Kennedy wanted to be a part of them.

A FAMILY TRADITION

Both Kennedy's grandfathers had been active in politics. Grandfather Fitzgerald, known as Honey Fitz, had been alderman, councilman, mayor of Boston, a state legislator, and a U.S. congressman. Grandfather Patrick Kennedy had been a state representative and a state senator. He had also been fire commissioner, street commissioner, and election commissioner of Boston. The family—particularly Joseph Kennedy Sr.—had assumed that Joe Jr. would carry on the family tradition and go into politics. Suddenly, John Kennedy was the oldest son of his generation, and that expectation fell on his shoulders. He felt that he had to fill his older brother's shoes, although he also felt that he could never do things quite as well as Joe would have done them.

Kennedy's chance to get into politics came when Congressman James Curley, a Democrat from the Eleventh

JAPAN SURRENDERS

As the war in Europe was winding down, Japan fought on, ignoring the Allies' calls for surrender. Finally, President Truman decided to use the atomic bomb to hasten the end of the war. U.S. bombers dropped the world's first atomic bomb on Hiroshima, Japan (below), on August 6, 1945, and the second on Nagasaki on August 9. The bombs caused terrible damage, but they did bring the war to an end. On September 2, Japan signed a formal treaty of surrender. World War II was over.

District of Massachusetts, decided to retire. The Eleventh District was a mix of factories, tenements, churches, saloons, shipping wharfs, and Harvard University. Kennedy declared his intention to run as a Democrat for Congress. He had connections with the old-line politicians through his father and grandfathers, but he also went to the people. Kennedy was friendly, but he was also shy and reserved. It wasn't easy for him to walk into a tavern or factory and talk to the workers, but he did it. Sometimes he'd get so involved in what they were doing and saying that he'd have to be pried away.

One of the people who opened his door to Jack was Dave Powers. Powers was just home from his war service and living with his widowed sister and her eight children in a run-down apartment in the Charlestown section of Boston. Powers was surprised when a tall, young stranger held out his hand and introduced himself. Kennedy said he was running for Congress and asked Powers to help.

Powers became one of Kennedy's hardest workers. He introduced Kennedy to people in the neighborhood and took him to meetings. Although Kennedy wasn't a great speaker, especially in front of large groups, people were impressed by his simplicity and sincerity. With men like Dave Powers, Larry O'Brien (a former Harvard football captain and one of Bobby Kennedy's teammates), and his brother Bobby, Kennedy set up groups of young Democrats throughout the district.

CONGRESSMAN KENNEDY

On election day, Kennedy and his proud Grandmother and Grandfather Fitzgerald walked to the polling place together. Jack won his congressional seat in 1946 by a

Kennedy and his grandparents, the Fitzgeralds, cast their votes in the 1946 congressional election. Kennedy won by a landslide.

margin of more than two to one. It put him on the front page of the *New York Times* and in *Time* magazine. He was twenty-nine years old, but looked younger than his age. In Congress he was sometimes mistaken for a Senate page or an elevator operator.

Kennedy served the people of his district faithfully. His office door was always open. Ted Reardon and a secretary named Mary Davis handled routine business in Congressman Kennedy's office, but often a telephone caller was surprised when the congressman himself answered.

Never a careful dresser, he often showed up for work wearing wrinkled trousers and mismatched socks. In contrast, another new congressman, Richard Nixon of California, was a very dapper dresser. They both served on the Education and Labor Committee.

As a new congressman, Kennedy didn't always know all he should have known about some issues. But he did have very strong opinions about social and economic issues, such as working conditions, wages, prices, Social Security, housing, aid to veterans and to the aged, and foreign policy. These issues represented the needs and concerns of the people he represented and the promises he had made during his election campaign. On these issues, Kennedy represented the new generation. Sometimes he even opposed President Truman, a fellow Democrat. Kennedy fought particularly hard for a bill to help make decent housing available to veterans. When veterans returned from the war, they faced an acute shortage of housing. But when housing legislation came up for a vote in Congress, Republicans and southern Democrats sided with the real estate and construction lobbies (groups who try to persuade politicians to vote a certain way). These members of Congress repeatedly defeated bills for low-rent housing projects. Kennedy often felt angry and frustrated.

Kennedy sometimes left his office early, put on a sweatshirt and sneakers, and played football or softball with a bunch of schoolkids at a Georgetown playground. One of the players told the coach that the new kid wasn't bad, but he needed a lot of work. Because Kennedy looked so young, it was hard for some older congressmen to take him seriously. Although the Kennedy name meant a lot in Boston, it wasn't very important—or even well known—in Washington.

A RACE FOR THE SENATE

After three two-year terms as a congressman, Kennedy became frustrated with House rules and customs. It was hard to dramatize his position on an issue, and legislation was often watered down to satisfy many different and opposing groups. He decided to run for the Senate in 1952. His opponent was Republican senator Henry Cabot Lodge from Massachusetts. Lodge had already served two terms in the Senate. He was fifteen years older than Kennedy and was a member of an old, distinguished family in Massachusetts. Honey Fitz had run unsuccessfully for the same Senate seat against Lodge's grandfather in 1916.

At the beginning of the 1952 campaign, Kennedy's back hurt so much that he was forced to use crutches. The hole left in his back from the last operation had never healed. He looked thin and sickly. His determination, however, was more intense than his pain. He had the will to win. This time he made twenty-seven-year-old Bobby Kennedy, who had just finished law school, his campaign manager. Except for Honey Fitz, who had died in 1950, the team that had worked so well before was together again.

The Kennedy campaign in Fall River, Massachusetts, was typical of Kennedy's style. The main industries in Fall River were textile making and women's clothing. Many of the residents were of French descent, and 90 percent of them were Republican. Kennedy made Ed Berube, a bus driver of French descent, his Fall River manager.

Because of his recurring back pain, Kennedy campaigned for the 1952 Senate election on crutches.

—————————— ✧

At the first Fall River political meeting, at a local church, Ed Berube stood up to announce the speaker, Congressman Joe Martin.

Martin was a Republican. The audience burst into laughter. Poor Ed Berube thought he was finished. Kennedy joined in the laughter and said that, although Ed might rather be working with Joe Martin, he'd rather have Berube working for him. Then Kennedy spoke to them in French and won their hearts.

Jack Kennedy was on a hectic schedule. He visited mills and factories, barbershops and small restaurants. He spoke to everyone he could. On one of his Fall River tours, he stopped at a small bakery run by "Babe" Piourde to buy some cupcakes. After tasting them, Kennedy told Piourde that if he ever got married, Piourde would bake the wedding cake.

Kennedy's sisters, Eunice, Patricia, and Jean, and often his mother, held teas at which Jack spoke. At one tea, a large group of women gathered on a hot July night. After his speech, Kennedy moved around the room to speak to each one of the women individually, although he was on crutches at the time.

Kennedy (left) *and Henry Cabot Lodge* (right)
share a handshake after the 1952 election.

SENATOR KENNEDY

When all the votes were in and tallied on election day in November 1952, Kennedy beat Lodge. Yet in a national wave of Republican support, Dwight D. Eisenhower won the presidency on the same day and carried Massachusetts by more than 200,000 votes. Eisenhower chose Lodge to be U.S. ambassador to the United Nations.

Shortly before his Senate campaign had begun, Kennedy was introduced to a beautiful young lady, Jacqueline Bouvier. She had grown up in New York and Washington and had attended Vassar College in New York and the Sorbonne in Paris, France. Her mother and stepfather lived in Newport, Rhode Island. Jacqueline's family was Catholic and came from a wealthy background. She spoke French, Italian, and Spanish fluently. Kennedy was much attracted to the soft-spoken, dark-haired Jacqueline, but he didn't see her again for six months. She went to Europe, and Kennedy was busy campaigning in Massachusetts.

After the election, Kennedy called Jacqueline. She had just returned to Washington and was working as an inquiring photographer—stopping people on the street to ask questions and take their photograph—for the *Times-Herald.* They began to see each other frequently. Finally, Kennedy asked her to marry him.

On September 12, 1953, they were married at St. Mary's Catholic Church in Newport, Rhode Island. Jacqueline's mother and stepfather were socially prominent and had a beautiful Newport estate, called Hammersmith Farm, where the wedding reception was held. The ceremony in the church was performed by Archbishop Richard Cushing of Boston, Rose Kennedy's good friend. Bobby Kennedy was the best man. True to his promise, Kennedy asked Babe Piourde to make the wedding cake.

Kennedy plunged into his Senate job with enthusiasm. He and Jacqueline moved into a red brick house in the Georgetown area of Washington. The front door opened onto a brick sidewalk. The back opened to a walled garden.

During the 1950s, the fear of Communism and Communist spy plots haunted the country. Anti-Communism was a popular political issue. While in the House of Representatives, Kennedy had persuaded labor representatives to testify about Communist influence within their unions. Kennedy served on the Senate Labor Committee and the Government Operations Committee, which was chaired by Senator Joe McCarthy of Wisconsin. McCarthy conducted congressional hearings to find out about Communist influence in the government, labor unions, and other organizations, but he turned the hearings into "witch hunts." McCarthy accused many innocent people of having Communist connections and ruined many lives and careers. As time went on, his charges became wilder and more unfounded. Eventually, a movement to officially censure (or criticize) McCarthy got under way in the Senate. This put Kennedy in a difficult spot, since his

✧ —————————

Joe McCarthy spent much of his career trying to expose Communists within the U.S. government. He ruined many lives, even though most of his claims were unfounded.

father supported McCarthy, and Jack Kennedy and Joe McCarthy had been freshman congressmen together.

On December 2, 1954, when the Senate voted on the matter, Kennedy was too sick to be there. His back had become extremely painful once more. He had also been diagnosed with Addison's disease, a glandular deficiency that lowers the body's resistance to infection. Jack had two delicate spinal operations, one in October 1954 and the other in February 1955.

While he was still flat on his back and recovering from the surgery, Jack wrote *Profiles in Courage.* This book shows the moral courage of eight senators who risked their careers for a great cause or a belief. Jacqueline visited him every day and was a great support to him.

— ✧ —

Kennedy signs copies of Profiles in Courage *for a group of fans.*

Profiles in Courage made the best-seller list, and in 1957 it won the Pulitzer Prize (an annual prize given for excellence in several categories of American literature) for Biography.

The day that Kennedy was able to return to his Senate office was a happy one for him. When he walked into the Senate chamber, all the senators stood and applauded to welcome him back. With a broad smile on his face, Kennedy took his seat in a back row.

One day, in the Senate caucus room, Senator Kennedy noticed a group of high school students in the hall. When he learned they were from Massachusetts, he invited them into the hearing room to observe congressional procedure firsthand.

Kennedy was beginning to make his mark in the Senate. He was well informed and able to see both sides of an issue. He weighed his decisions carefully. For this he was sometimes called a "cold fish," meaning he didn't feel strongly about anything. But that was far from the truth.

Kennedy believed strongly in the right of every person to get a good education, to have an equal opportunity for jobs, and to have a decent standard of living. On May 17, 1954, the Supreme Court had handed down its famous decision on school desegregation. In *Brown v. Board of Education of Topeka,* the Court ruled that segregation in public schools was unconstitutional. There could no longer be separate schools for black children. Enforcement of the decision moved very slowly, hardly at all in the southern states. Southern Democratic senators and conservative Republicans voted down any meaningful, new civil rights legislation.

CHAPTER FIVE

ON HIS WAY

"For there is a new world to be won—a world
of hope and abundance. And I want America to
lead the way to that new world."
—John F. Kennedy, in a television address,
July 4, 1960

At the 1956 Democratic National Convention in Chicago, Jack Kennedy was considered a possible candidate for vice president. He made the nominating speech for Adlai Stevenson, who was again running as the Democratic presidential candidate against President Dwight D. Eisenhower. It was Jack Kennedy's first nationwide television appearance. He did well, but Senator Estes Kefauver of Tennessee became the Democratic candidate for vice president.

Kennedy went back to his job in the Senate. He had renewed determination to do the best he could possibly do, as his father had always taught him.

Kennedy began speaking to groups all over the country. In six weeks during the fall of 1956, he made more than 150 speeches and appearances and traveled in twenty-four states. At first he campaigned for Adlai Stevenson, but after Stevenson's defeat in November, he continued his speeches on his own behalf. He wanted to visit every state in the country. It was no secret that Kennedy had his eye on the presidency.

Jacqueline didn't like the frantic pace of campaigning or the way a campaign disrupted family life. She knew that Kennedy would have to be away from home even more than his usual Senate business required. Jacqueline disliked being alone so much of the time, but she didn't want to discourage her husband, so she tried to do her part.

In his second term in the Senate, Kennedy quickly assumed a position of leadership. He became a member of the powerful Senate Foreign Relations Committee in 1957. He was also chairman of the Senate Subcommittee on Labor. He was known as a young man in a hurry. His office, crowded with people, books, papers, posters, and souvenirs of PT 109, seemed to be one of the busiest spots in Washington. Somehow, among all the hustle and bustle, the work got done.

Late in 1957, the Kennedys' hopes for a child were answered when Caroline was born. The quiet, three-story home in Georgetown had a nursery, a baby carriage, and a proud father. Kennedy delighted in each stage of Caroline's development. With the birth of Caroline, Jacqueline seemed happier than ever before in her married life. She was a radiant young mother.

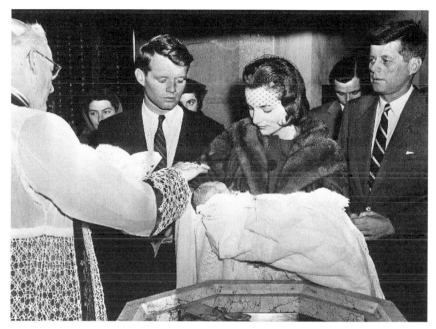

Caroline Kennedy was christened on December 13, 1957. Jackie's sister,
Lee, holds Caroline while Bobby (left) and John (right) look on.

——————— ✧ ———————

Kennedy and his brother Bobby found themselves more
and more in the news in the late 1950s. Bobby Kennedy was
chief counsel for the Senate Investigations Subcommittee,
chaired by Senator John McClellan. When this committee
uncovered corrupt labor practices, a new subcommittee,
sometimes called the Rackets Committee, was formed to
look into the matter more closely. McClellan and Bobby
Kennedy carried over their roles to the new subcommittee.
Because Jack Kennedy was on the Senate Labor Committee,
he was chosen as one of four senators on the new subcommittee. Both brothers worked closely together and became
known to the public during the televised hearings.

John (second from right) *and Robert* (second from left) *Kennedy*
participated in the McClellan hearings to investigate corrupt labor practices.

———————————————— ✧ ————————————————

John Kennedy was emerging as a person in his own
right. It had taken a long time to rid himself of the belief
that he was only a poor substitute for his brother Joe.
But he was no longer in Joe's shadow. In fact, he had
many qualities that Joe had lacked. He was known for his
sharp wit, his remarkable command of facts, and—best of
all—his ability to laugh at himself. He cared passionately
about poor people, old people, and victims of unfairness
all over the country and the world. He had tried to help
these people through legislation. Then he decided to try
for a more powerful job—that of the president. He
thought that, as president, he would have a much better
chance of reaching his goals.

He started taking novocaine injections to reduce his back pain and a new medication to help control his Addison's disease. His health had improved. No one would think that the smiling, handsome, confident young man was in pain.

Over the next few years, Jack talked to coal miners in West Virginia, dairy farmers in Wisconsin, labor leaders in Chicago, politicians in New York. Everywhere he went, he found his Catholic religion raised doubt and suspicion in voters. People were afraid that the pope, who resides in Rome, Italy, and is the head of the Catholic Church, would run the United States if a Catholic were elected. No Catholic had ever been president. Only one Catholic had ever run for that office—Al Smith of New York—and he had been soundly beaten in 1928.

At a meeting held at a high school in a far western state, the matter came into the open. A student stood up and asked Senator Kennedy if a Catholic could become president.

Kennedy replied that he had taken an oath of loyalty to his country when he entered the navy, when he became a congressman, and when he became a senator. "If I was qualified to serve my country in those other capacities, I am qualified to serve it as president." He added, "No one asked my brother Joe if he had divided loyalties when he volunteered and died for his country." The audience applauded his answer.

By 1959 the campaign was running in high gear. Kennedy bought a plane (called the *Caroline* after his daughter) so he would always have rapid transportation. His campaign staff was working smoothly. His manager was Bobby Kennedy. Ted Sorensen, Larry O'Brien, Ken O'Donnell, Dave Powers, Steve Smith (later his sister Jean's husband), and Pierre Salinger (recently added as press secretary) also played important roles.

THE PRESIDENTIAL PRIMARIES

The presidential primary elections began early in March in New Hampshire, where Kennedy won with a record vote. Primary elections test the voters' preference for a presidential candidate. Two or more candidates of the same political party compete for votes. In many states, winning a primary election means a candidate wins the pledges of delegates to the national convention, where the party's presidential nominee is selected. Kennedy knew he needed those delegate votes.

RELIGION TEST

The fifty-member Council of Methodist Bishops met in Washington in April 1959 and invited Kennedy to attend. There he was quizzed on his religion and its possible effect on his ability to hold office.

"I am a strong Catholic," Kennedy replied. "I come from a strong Catholic family. But I regret the fact that some people get the idea that the Catholic Church favors a church-state tie. I will make my decisions according to my own judgment of the best interests of all people. I do not intend to disavow [give up] either my religion or my beliefs in order to win the presidency. If the outcome of this campaign was settled on the day I was born, then the whole nation is the loser."

The bishops applauded his talk. They admitted that they admired his honesty, courage, and his impartial attitude. It was quite a victory for Kennedy.

Democratic senator Hubert Humphrey of Minnesota also wanted to be president. He entered the Wisconsin primary. Kennedy decided to challenge him there. Bobby Kennedy advised his brother not to do it. Humphrey was very well known in Wisconsin. Not only are Wisconsin and Minnesota neighboring states, they also share many similarities. For example, both are dairy and farming states. Jack Kennedy was in no sense a farm boy. The religious question was also a big obstacle since many residents of both states are of Protestant German and Scandinavian descent. Kennedy went ahead with his plan. In bitter, wintry cold he walked the streets of small towns in Wisconsin. At first, people seemed to disappear as he approached. Everyone knew that Kennedy was a rich man's son. He flew in on his own plane. Humphrey came on a bus.

Gradually, the picture changed. Crowds kept getting larger. People began to realize that this "rich man's son" cared about them. He was informed about the problems of the farmer, the small dairy operator, and people in small businesses. People said that he had a "good head on his shoulders." He cared about the unemployed and about decent wages and living conditions. On primary day, April 5, 1960, Wisconsin Democrats chose Kennedy as their presidential candidate over Humphrey by 106,000 votes.

Kennedy and Humphrey were opponents again in the West Virginia primary. The state faced pressing problems of poverty, unemployment, and health care. And in a state where only 3 percent of the population were Catholic, the religious issue was very important to the voters. Kennedy had to answer questions about his religion again and again.

On May 10, when West Virginians went to the polls, they gave Kennedy 212,000 votes to 136,000 for Humphrey. Humphrey withdrew as a presidential candidate. Kennedy continued a strenuous schedule of speaking engagements from one end of the country to the other.

Senator Humphrey was out of the running, but a number of other prominent Democrats were giving Kennedy strong competition. Among them were Senator Stuart Symington of Missouri, Senator Lyndon Johnson of Texas, and Governor Pat Brown of California.

THE NATIONAL CONVENTIONS

Several weeks before the Democratic convention, the Republican Party held its convention. Republican delegates

———————————— ✧ ————————————

Hubert Humphrey (right) was among the Democratic presidential hopefuls in the 1960 election, but he lost the primaries to Kennedy.

Richard Nixon (right) was the Republican candidate in the 1960 presidential election.

had nominated Richard Nixon, Eisenhower's vice president, as their 1960 presidential candidate. Nixon and Kennedy had been freshman congressmen together.

The 1960 Democratic National Convention in Los Angeles, California, was noisy and colorful. Behind all the carnival atmosphere, serious men and women were weighing the merits and chances of their candidates. The candidates spoke to delegates from the various states to explain their views. Kennedy refused to change any of his positions to please a particular group. He was his own man. Not even Kennedy's father could sway his views.

Balloting, or voting for the candidates, began in the Los Angeles Sports Arena. The states were called on to vote, one by one, in alphabetical order. The magic number was 761— the number of votes a nominee needed to win the presidential nomination. Bobby Kennedy and Larry O'Brien estimated that Kennedy had a sure 762 votes. But nothing is sure during a presidential convention. Delegates could always change their votes.

In all the noise and banner waving, the straw hats and printed slogans, the voice of the person calling the roll boomed out over the public address system: "Wyoming!"

Kennedy needed only eleven more votes to win. Ten of Wyoming's fifteen votes were pledged to him. Younger brother Ted Kennedy had been campaigning in the western states. He quickly worked his way through the crowd to the Wyoming delegation to remind the delegates of the important role they could play. Wyoming cast all fifteen of its votes for Kennedy, putting him over the top!

The final vote for Kennedy was 806, and the convention voted to make it unanimous. Most of the family were there, except Jacqueline, who was expecting another baby, and Kennedy's father, who had tried to stay in the background during the campaign. Kennedy's sister Patricia tossed her hat in the air. Teddy grabbed the Wyoming standard and waved it wildly. Rose Kennedy smiled proudly.

Jack Kennedy had watched the proceedings on television in a rented apartment. It was customary for candidates not to appear on the floor of the convention until results were final. Kennedy's car had to inch its way through cheering crowds, reporters, and photographers. A huge traffic jam developed, and it wasn't until the early morning of July 12 that he was able to join the rest of the family at the Sports Arena.

People were crying with joy as Kennedy made his brief acceptance speech. He said, "This is in many ways the most important election in the history of our country. All of us are united in our devotion to this country. We wish to keep it strong and free. It requires the best in all of us. I can assure all of you here who have reposed this confidence in me that I'll be worthy of your trust."

The convention wasn't over yet. A vice presidential candidate had to be chosen. Lyndon B. Johnson had been

By 1960 Kennedy had long outgrown his shyness in public speaking.
Here he gives his acceptance speech at the Democratic
National Convention in Los Angeles, California.

———————————— ✧ ————————————

Kennedy's closest rival, with 409 votes. Kennedy felt sure
that Johnson would be the strongest running mate. As a
senator from Texas, Johnson commanded a large number of
votes in the general election, because in 1960 Texas was the
largest state in the Union. Jack also hoped that the selec-
tion of Johnson might influence some southern and western
states. But Bobby Kennedy and many others were against
choosing Johnson as the vice presidential candidate.

The next day, all the convention delegates and party leaders were on hand to unite behind their new leader, John

Lyndon Johnson (left) agreed to be Kennedy's vice presidential running mate.
✧ ————————————

Fitzgerald Kennedy. He chose Johnson to be his vice president. The delegates ratified, or confirmed, his choice. Johnson said, "I had no right to say that I would refuse to serve in any capacity."

When Kennedy addressed the convention, he introduced the idea of the "New Frontier."

The New Frontier is here, whether we seek it or not. . . . I believe that the times require imagination and courage and perseverance. I'm asking each of you to be pioneers toward the New Frontier. My call is to the young in heart, regardless of age—to the stout in spirit, regardless of party, to all who respond to the scriptural call, "Be strong and of courage, be not afraid, neither be dismayed."

CHAPTER SIX

"ASK WHAT YOU CAN DO...."

"Let the word go forth from this time and place, to friend and foe alike, that the torch has been passed to a new generation of Americans...."
—John Kennedy, inaugural address, January 20, 1961

During the campaign, Jack Kennedy endured eighteen-hour days. He made brief personal appearances in many small communities and wrote speeches while traveling on the *Caroline*. In ten weeks, he traveled 78,654 miles. Everywhere he went, the crowds got bigger.

Toward the end of the campaign, a series of four televised debates between Kennedy and Nixon took place. These were the first televised presidential political debates ever to be held. They gave the American public a chance to see and compare both candidates. At the first debate, held in a Chicago television studio, Nixon looked stiff and ill at ease. Nixon presented his ideas well enough, but he did not answer Kennedy's arguments in a convincing way.

In 1960 presidential candidates debated on national television for the first time. This family watches one such debate between Kennedy and Nixon.

———————— ✧ ————————

Kennedy had the advantage of spontaneity, of being able to ad-lib with ease. All the practice he had had in answering questions from high school and college audiences, crowds of coal miners, farmers, and Protestant ministers had sharpened his naturally quick mind. He had facts and figures to back up his arguments. He was no longer the shy young man who hesitantly addressed small groups of Massachusetts voters. He had poise, ease, and wit. His sincerity impressed TV audiences. The debates marked a turning point in the campaign.

Kennedy's last appearance of the campaign was at a huge rally in the Boston Gardens on the eve of the election. In his speech there, he said, "I ask you to join us in all the tomorrows yet to come, in building America, moving America, picking this country of ours up and sending it into the '60s."

The next morning, November 8, 1960, John and Jacqueline Kennedy were at the polls early to cast their votes in Boston, still their legal residence. Then they took a plane to Hyannis Port, where press and television headquarters had been set up at Bobby Kennedy's house.

Election results were slow coming in. For the first time, computers were being used on a large scale to count votes. At 7:15 A.M. news commentators predicted a lopsided victory for Richard Nixon. An hour later, they predicted a Kennedy sweep. Kennedy and his loyal workers refused to take these early predictions seriously. The eastern states were the first to be heard from. Around midnight Kennedy had a lead of 2.3 million. Slowly, that lead went down. As returns from the West and Midwest came in, the picture became more confused. All the Kennedys except Jacqueline stood around at Bobby's house, tense and silent. Jacqueline, expecting the baby soon, stayed in her own Hyannis Port home.

Kennedy finally began to gain in electoral votes. (The candidate who gets the most votes within a state wins all of that state's electoral votes. The number of votes a state has is based on its population.) At 3:00 A.M., word came that Nixon would make an appearance at the Ambassador Hotel in Los Angeles. The group at Bobby's house all thought that Nixon would concede the election to Kennedy. Instead, Nixon said, "If the present trend continues, Mr.—Senator Kennedy will be the next president of the United States."

At 4:00 A.M., everyone went to bed. In the morning, there was still no definite word. The only one who was sure of the outcome was young Caroline. When she first saw her father that morning she said, "Good morning, Mr. President." Kennedy laughed and then took his daughter down to the beach.

Although the day was cold and windy, almost all of the Kennedys were out that morning walking along the bleak shore of the Atlantic Ocean. Secret Service men appeared about 7:30 A.M., and Jack took that as a good sign. Secret Service men were always assigned to guard the president.

The family and close friends went back to Bobby's house and grouped around the television. Around noon Minnesota came through for Kennedy. The long wait was over. Kennedy had won!

Nixon sent a telegram of congratulations, saying in part, "I know you will have the support of all Americans as you lead the nation in the cause of peace and freedom in the next four years."

Kennedy could acknowledge his victory and thank all those who had worked so hard for him and all those who had voted for him. He and Jacqueline and all the Kennedys, campaign workers, friends, and supporters went to the Hyannis Port National Guard Armory, where the press and fans were waiting. Kennedy made a brief speech, read the telegrams of congratulations from Nixon and President Eisenhower, and finished with, "So now my wife and I prepare for a new administration—and for a new baby."

The president-elect and his wife returned to Georgetown, she to await the baby, he to begin forming his staff and cabinet (advisors). He put his sister Eunice's husband, Sargent Shriver, aide Larry O'Brien, and his brother to work seeking out the best possible choices for important posts in the new

Chief Justice Earl Warren swears in members of Kennedy's cabinet.

✧

administration. He also consulted some of his former Harvard professors. He said that he wanted the best men he could find.

In the weeks between the November election and the January inauguration, Jacqueline gave birth to a baby boy. They called him John Fitzgerald Kennedy Jr. As soon as John Jr. was strong enough to travel, Jack, Jacqueline, Caroline, and "Caroline's baby brother" went to Palm Beach, Florida, for the Christmas holidays.

When Kennedy and his family returned to Georgetown, shortly before the inauguration, reporters besieged the front door of their red brick house at all hours. To spare Jacqueline and the rest of the household, Kennedy got into the habit of meeting reporters at the front door with each announcement of a new appointee. He would stand, hatless and coatless, in the wintry weather, and with his usual good humor answer their questions.

Kennedy chose people based on their intelligence and integrity rather than on their party loyalty. He asked Robert McNamara, a Republican, to be secretary of defense, and Douglas Dillon, another Republican, to be secretary of the treasury.

The only appointment Kennedy hesitated to announce to reporters was that of his brother Bobby. Kennedy wanted no one else as attorney general of the United States. But his brother was not easy to persuade. "Come over and have breakfast with me," Kennedy told him. "Come and see the new baby."

After he had admired John Jr. in his crib, Bobby protested that people would object to the appointment. Kennedy joked that he'd make the announcement about 2:00 A.M., when no one would be around.

Both brothers met the press, and Jack Kennedy made the announcement. Immediately, they were hit with just the kinds of questions and remarks they had feared. Kennedy explained that he trusted his brother more

——————————— ✧

When Kennedy appointed his brother Robert (right) attorney general, many wondered if Robert was truly fit for the job.

than anyone else he could think of—trusted his judgment, his ability, and his commitment. When the two Kennedys went back into the house, the reporters all trooped across the street to the house of a kind woman who often served them coffee and doughnuts while they warmed up.

INAUGURATION DAY

The night before inauguration day, it snowed heavily. Cars were stranded in snowdrifts. Many people walked in snow over their ankles. But somehow everyone made it to their destinations. It all added to the spirit of adventure and excitement that everyone felt.

On the morning of inauguration day, Kennedy went across the street to the kind woman's house. The walks had not yet been shoveled. Great was the woman's surprise when she opened the door and found the bareheaded president-elect with a bronze plaque under his arm. He had had it made for her to commemorate her kindness to the cold, hungry reporters. He also sent a special car to take her to the inauguration, where he had reserved a seat for her. He then continued on to his parish church, Holy Trinity, for Mass.

With cheering crowds lining the still snowy streets, John and Jacqueline Kennedy left Georgetown to have coffee with the Eisenhowers. Although the president-elect had requested all the men to wear formal attire, he carried his top hat and only once in a while remembered to put it on. The old and new presidential parties arrived at the Capitol steps around 12:30 P.M. With his right hand on the family Bible, John Kennedy swore to uphold the Constitution and the laws of the United States to the best of his ability.

Before he gave his inaugural address, Kennedy looked out over the vast crowd of foreign dignitaries, family, friends, ordinary people, and government officials. Then he introduced the frail, white-haired old man who stood nearby, poet Robert Frost.

The poet took a few steps forward to face the microphone. The wind ruffled his wispy, white hair. The wintry sun glanced off the white paper he held in his hand and blinded him. The paper shook as his hand trembled. The young president who had invited him smiled encouragingly. Robert Frost, in a voice suddenly strong, lay down the troublesome paper and recited from memory another poem,

——————————— ❖ ———————————

*The poet Robert Frost recites "The Gift Outright" at
President Kennedy's inauguration on January 20, 1961.*

"The Gift Outright"—"The land was ours before we were the land's. . . ."

When Frost finished his poem, Jack stepped to the podium to deliver his inaugural address. His face solemn, his voice ringing with conviction, the new president began:

My fellow Americans: We observe today not a
     victory of party but a celebration of freedom,
     symbolizing an end as well as a beginning,
     signifying renewal as well as change. . . .
We dare not forget today that we are the heirs of that
     first revolution. Let the word go forth from this
     time and place, to friend and foe alike, that the
     torch had been passed to a new generation of
     Americans, . . . unwilling to witness or permit the
     slow undoing of those human rights to which this
     nation has always been committed. . . .
In your hands, my fellow citizens, more than mine,
     will rest the final success or failure of our course.
     Since this country was founded, each generation
     of Americans has been summoned to give
     testimony to its national loyalty. The graves of
     young Americans who answered the call to service
     surround the globe.
Now the trumpet summons us again—not as a call
     to bear arms, though arms we need; not as a call
     to battle, though embattled we are; but as a call
     to bear the burden of a long twilight struggle, year
     in and year out, . . . a struggle against the
     common enemies of man: tyranny, poverty,
     disease and war itself. . . .

*And so, my fellow Americans: ask not what your
country can do for you; ask what you can do for
your country. . . .*

To the audience before him and to millions of people watching on television, this new, young president embodied a fresh spirit, new ideas, dedication, and hope for great things to come.

A huge parade filled the rest of the afternoon. Kennedy was thrilled by a PT 109 float with Leonard Thom, Barney Ross, and other wartime buddies grinning and waving. That evening at the inaugural ball, Jacqueline looked beautiful in her white gown. She left the festivities around midnight, but Kennedy stayed much later, moving from one event to another and plainly having a good time.

CHAPTER SEVEN

THE NEW FRONTIER

"The New Frontier of which I speak is not a set of promises—it is a set of challenges. It sums up not what I intend to offer the American people, but what I intend to ask of them."
—John Kennedy, accepting the Democratic presidential nomination on July 15, 1960

When the excitement and thrill of inauguration day ended, Kennedy lost no time in getting down to business. He called a meeting his first morning in office, January 21, 1961. He was waiting in the Oval Office when Presidential Aide Ted Sorensen, Special Assistant Arthur Schlesinger Jr., Press Secretary Pierre Salinger, Appointments Secretary Kenny O'Donnell, Larry O'Brien, and Dave Powers arrived. Larry O'Brien was Kennedy's contact with the House and Senate regarding legislation. Dave Powers was his personal aide.

LIFE AT THE WHITE HOUSE

A big change in lifestyle took place at the White House when the Kennedys moved in. White House dinners became occasions at which wit, culture, and sparkling intellect were the order of the evening. The Kennedys were gracious hosts, and they set the pace for lively discussions. At one dinner in honor of Nobel Prize winners *(above)*, Kennedy said, "I think this is the most extraordinary collection of talent, of human knowledge, that has ever been gathered together at the White House—with the possible exception of when Thomas Jefferson dined alone."

Jacqueline wanted to restore the White House to its former charm and dignity. She asked the people of the United

States to help her find antiques that might once have been part of the mansion's furnishings. People responded from all over the land.

A busy president, Kennedy also found time to romp with his children. One of John Jr.'s favorite games was one he made up himself. He hid behind the movable panel in his father's desk *(below)*. Jack had to rap on the panel and ask if the bunny was home. John Jr. then jumped out, a delighted smile on his face, while his father acted surprised. Sometimes Caroline, dressed in her mother's high heels, popped in on a meeting. Life at the Kennedy White House was never dull.

Many problems faced the new president. Kennedy was concerned about the poor and hungry of all races. One out of every sixteen workers in the country was unemployed. Fewer high school and college students were finding jobs. Kennedy often substituted executive orders (acts or regulations carried out by the president) for legislation that would not pass or would be slow to pass in Congress. He felt that some problems were too important for help to be delayed or blocked by political maneuvering.

On his first working day as president, Kennedy signed an executive order doubling the amount of government surplus food distributed to millions of jobless Americans and their families. He knew that distributing food was not the answer to hunger and poverty. It was only a short-term measure until more lasting solutions could be found. He also expanded the Food for Peace program to help starving people in other countries. On January 30, he asked Congress to include health insurance in the Social Security program. The health insurance plan was called Medicare in the bill (legislation) he sent to Congress. Although he worked hard to get the Medicare bill passed, it was defeated 52–48 in the Senate.

Kennedy was always interested in the welfare of young people. He started the President's Council on Physical Fitness, a program to encourage boys and girls to keep fit and healthy. Soon not only young people but people of every age were out jogging or walking to improve their fitness and well-being.

THE PEACE CORPS

One of President Kennedy's favorite projects was the Peace Corps, which he set up by executive order. Its

Kennedy established the Peace Corps to promote peace and friendship between the United States and other nations. Here he greets a group of Peace Corps volunteers.

purpose was to promote world peace and friendship. Recruitment and training of volunteers began in the spring of 1961. On September 22, 1961, Congress officially established the Peace Corps. Volunteers were mostly young people who wanted to share their skills and energy with the people of poor nations. Peace Corps volunteers taught school, built roads, bridges, schools, and health centers and developed farming skills—whatever was most needed. Their job was to help people in underdeveloped lands help themselves.

The Peace Corps gave people in South America, Central America, Africa, and Asia a new idea of the United States. Volunteers lived and worked under the same conditions as the people around them. They learned and spoke the language of the people they were working with, and they went only to countries where they were invited. Peace Corps volunteers really cared about helping people, and they liked what they were doing. David Crozier, a Peace Corps volunteer in Colombia, wrote to his parents, "Should it come to it, I had rather give my life trying to help someone than to have to give my life looking down a gun barrel at them."

The Peace Corps began with five hundred volunteers. A year and a half later, nearly five thousand Peace Corps volunteers were working in forty-five countries around the world.

CIVIL RIGHTS

Not all of President Kennedy's undertakings met with such success. A coalition (or alliance) of southern Democrats and Republican conservatives in Congress blocked every civil rights bill.

At first, Kennedy carried out his civil rights plan by executive order. He was aware of the unjust treatment of black people in the United States, especially in the South at the time. He wanted not only to eliminate discrimination but also to teach people that discrimination was wrong. As a congressman and senator, Kennedy had voted for every civil rights bill that had been introduced. In his first debate with Richard Nixon during the presidential campaign, he had said:

The [African American] baby born in America today. . . has about one-half as much chance of

*completing high school as a white baby...
one-third as much chance of completing
college...twice as much chance of becoming
unemployed...a life expectancy which is seven
years shorter, and the prospects of earning only
one-half as much.*

Kennedy and his brother had always worked closely together, and they continued to do so during the nation's struggle for civil rights. Bobby Kennedy and other Department of Justice officials carried out quiet meetings with school boards in Atlanta, Dallas, Memphis, New Orleans, and other southern cities. As a result, many schools were integrated with a minimum of fuss. Railroads, bus stations, and airlines followed a similar pattern.

Although the president could not persuade Congress to pass the civil rights laws he wanted, he used litigation (lawsuits), negotiation, persuasion, executive orders, directives, and personal actions as powerful tools in the cause of civil rights. Kennedy publicly endorsed the principle of equal rights, and he was able to force many small but significant changes in policy that set a whole new tone.

For example, Kennedy directed people in his administration to refuse to speak before segregated audiences, and they were directed to boycott segregated private clubs. U.S. employment offices were told to refuse job orders "for whites only." When Kennedy spoke at press club dinners, black faces were among the formerly all-white audience. Black as well as white members of the Secret Service guarded the president, and blacks were included in the pool of White House drivers.

THE CIVIL RIGHTS MOVEMENT

The civil rights movement was in full swing when Kennedy took office. Under the leadership of Martin Luther King Jr., African Americans—joined by many northern whites—were nonviolently protesting against segregated public facilities (such as restaurants, stores, and schools) and other unjust treatment.

In 1961 Freedom Riders rode buses to different southern towns and cities to test the enforcement of desegregation in public facilities. Freedom Riders were mostly young people, both black and white, from many parts of the United States.

Many people did not agree with the views of the Freedom Riders. This Freedom Riders bus was set on fire by angry protesters in 1961.

Freedom riders were often attacked and beaten while the police stood and watched. Kennedy—and his brother as attorney general—frequently sent federal troops *(above)* to protect King, peaceful protesters, and black students from angry white mobs. In response to the situation, President Kennedy addressed the nation on television. He said:

> *Our nation is founded on the principle that observance of the law is the eternal safeguard of liberty. . . . Even among law-abiding men, few laws are universally loved, but they are uniformly respected and not resisted. Americans are free to disagree with the law, but not to disobey it. For in a government of laws and not of men, no man, however prominent and powerful, and no mob, however unruly or boisterous, is entitled to defy a court of law. . . .*

On June 11, 1963, the president decided to address the nation about civil rights. He committed himself and the country "to the proposition that race has no place in American life or law." He talked about legislation he would send to Congress, but he also said that "Legislation cannot solve the problem alone. It must be solved in the homes of every American." He pointed out the moral injustice of racial discrimination. "We are confronted primarily with a moral issue. . . . Now the time has come for this nation to fulfill its promise. . . . Those who do nothing are inviting shame as well as violence. Those who act boldly are recognizing right as well as reality."

On June 19, the president sent to Congress the broadest U.S. civil rights bill ever proposed. In his message, he said that simple justice required this program "not merely for reasons of economic efficiency, world diplomacy and domestic tranquility—but, above all, because it is right."

On August 28, 1963, a unique event took place: the historic March on Washington. People, both blacks and whites, from all over the country, 250,000 strong, marched from the Washington Monument to the Lincoln Memorial in support of civil rights. It was the largest public demonstration that had ever been held in Washington. People marveled at the spirit and self-discipline of the marchers. The crowd was quiet and orderly. Many people listened with tears in their eyes as they heard Martin Luther King's ringing words: "I have a dream that my four little children will one day live in a nation where they will be judged not by the color of their skin, but by the content of their character. . . . I have a dream," he cried again and again, describing the day when peace and equality would prevail.

*Martin Luther King Jr. addresses the crowd during
the March on Washington on August 28, 1963.*

——————————— ✧ ———————————

After the march, several prominent black leaders were invited to the White House to talk to the president. Kennedy met them and led them to his private quarters. When he learned that most of them hadn't had a chance to eat all day, he had food brought in. They discussed with the president ways to bring about the reforms they so badly needed. When they left, they felt that Jack Kennedy was a strong fighter on their side.

CHAPTER EIGHT

FOREIGN POLICY

"Let every nation know, whether it wishes us well or ill, that we shall pay any price, bear any burden, meet any hardship, support any friend, oppose any foe to assure the survival and the success of liberty."

—John Kennedy, inaugural address, January 20, 1961

One of President Kennedy's worst failures happened shortly after he took office. The large island of Cuba, just ninety miles south of Florida, had fallen into Communist hands. In 1959 Fidel Castro and a band of rebels had overthrown the government of dictator Fulgencio Batista. Under Castro's leadership, Cuba became a Communist country. Its government allows only one political party—the Cuban Communist Party.

The U.S. government was concerned about having a Communist neighbor, so some government officials had decided to mount an attack. The plan would use 1,400 Cuban exiles (those living outside of Cuba), called the Cuban Brigade.

Although the Central Intelligence Agency (CIA) was in charge of this plan, the whole action was to be the work of the Cubans themselves. It was thought that, once the Cuban Brigade had landed, the Cuban people would rise up in revolt and support it. The Bay of Pigs in Cuba was to be the landing place.

When former president Eisenhower first told Kennedy of the plan, he was appalled. He quickly called a meeting of his advisers. Allen Dulles and Richard Bissel, both of the CIA, General Lyman L. Lemnitzer, chairman of the Joint Chiefs of Staff, and Admiral Arleigh Burke, chief of naval operations, all advised Kennedy to go ahead with the plan.

Kennedy had his doubts. Other members of his staff also felt unsure about the wisdom of the plan, but they didn't speak out very forcefully. Dulles and Bissel urged haste and secrecy. Kennedy reluctantly gave his consent.

On April 17, 1961, the invasion began. The planners were not familiar with conditions at the Bay of Pigs. The invasion became an incredible series of blunders due to faulty information about Castro's military strength. Castro's small air force sank two U.S. freighters carrying ammunition, communication equipment, food, and medical supplies, and the anti-Castro force of B-26 planes was shot down. Supplies never reached the Cuban exiles on the beach.

The Cuban underground, a secret group in Cuba that was supposed to have rallied the Cuban people to support the invaders, never knew about the plan. Without supplies, ammunition, arms, or air cover, Cuban Brigade 2506 fought on bravely until they were killed or captured.

The doomed venture came to an end on April 19. Although it had been an Eisenhower project that Kennedy

The Bay of Pigs invasion was a military and political disaster.
Here Kennedy meets with veterans of the doomed operation.

had inherited, he refused to let anyone in his administration make excuses for him. He said, "I am the responsible
officer of the government and that is quite obvious." He
did learn a lesson from the experience. From then on, however, he made sure to examine all sides of a question, and
he never again made a decision hastily.

ALLIANCE FOR PROGRESS

That same spring, Kennedy set up the Alliance for Progress
to help form stronger ties between the United States and
South and Central America. Most of the countries of
South America were ruled by dictators. The people had no
voice in government. Wealthy landowners lived in luxury,
while the rest of the population lived in misery. Much the
same conditions existed in Central America. Kennedy

wanted to do something to relieve the poverty of the people and to reform their dictatorial systems.

Later that year, the Kennedys went to Venezuela and Colombia. Just three years before, crowds in Lima, Peru, and Caracas, Venezuela, had thrown stones at and spit on Vice President Richard Nixon and his wife. The Kennedys, however, were greeted by cheering crowds. In Bogotá, Colombia, Kennedy outlined a plan for democratic reform, economic development, and a united front against poverty and oppression. In an open field near Bogotá, Kennedy dedicated a future housing project. A year later, he received a grateful letter from the first family to move into the project. The letter stated, "We are very happy to . . . no longer be moving around like outcasts. Now we have dignity and freedom."

MEETINGS IN EUROPE

Another problem requiring Kennedy's attention was how to deal with Premier Nikita Khrushchev, the Communist leader of the Soviet Union. Khrushchev invited President Kennedy to meet with him in Vienna, Austria, in early June 1961. Kennedy wanted to meet Khrushchev so that they might understand each other better. Jacqueline accompanied her husband to Europe.

Before going to Austria, the Kennedys visited President Charles de Gaulle of France. France wanted to develop its own atomic bomb. Jack hoped to persuade President de Gaulle that the fewer nations with the bomb, the safer all nations would be.

The Kennedys also stopped in Great Britain. Kennedy met with British prime minister Harold Macmillan. He also paid his first and only visit to the grave of his beloved

In June 1961, President Kennedy met with three of Europe's key leaders:
Soviet premier Nikita Khrushchev (left)*, French president Charles de*
Gaulle (center)*, and British prime minister Harold Macmillan* (right)*.*

"Kicks," his sister Kathleen, who had been killed in an airplane accident over France and had been buried in Britain.

At their meeting in Austria, Kennedy and Khrushchev faced the problem of two great enemy nations trying to avoid war. Two points of disagreement hinged on the requirements for creating a nuclear test ban treaty (an agreement to stop tests of nuclear weapons) and the presence of Western troops in Berlin.

At the end of World War II, Germany had been divided into sectors (zones) controlled by the Allied forces: Great Britain, France, the Soviet Union, and the United States. The city of Berlin, the capital of Germany at that time, was located in what became the Soviet zone. But because the city was so important, it too was divided into sectors. The Soviets controlled East Berlin. West Berlin was under the control of Britain, France, and the

United States. Military troops stayed there to protect and maintain the established sectors.

Khrushchev wanted all but the Soviet troops out of Berlin. But leaving would have meant abandoning about two million West Berliners, allowing them to fall under East German Communist control. President Kennedy refused to do that.

Also, the Soviet Union would not agree to inspection of its nuclear test sites. Without inspection, the United States would have no way of knowing whether the Soviet Union would be obeying the rules of the proposed test ban treaty. The two leaders did come to a tentative agreement on other issues, and they made a joint statement promising to keep in contact with each other.

THE MISSILE CRISIS

On Tuesday morning, October 16, 1962, Kennedy was having breakfast when McGeorge Bundy, his national security adviser, called on him. What Bundy had to tell him was shocking. The U.S. government had photos showing that the Soviet Union was building missile sites in Cuba.

For months Soviet ships had been delivering mysterious equipment to Cuba. When asked about this, Anatoly Dobrynin, Soviet ambassador to the United States, had said that the Soviets were only sending defensive weapons and equipment in case the United States attacked Cuba. However, photos taken by U.S. planes showed Soviet missile sites close to completion. The missiles were weapons of aggression, not defense.

Kennedy was outwardly calm and cool, but privately he was furious with Khrushchev for deceiving him. He quickly set up a meeting of top officials and trusted friends and advisers. The group became known as the Executive Committee. The press dubbed it ExCom. John McCone, head of the CIA, Attorney General Robert Kennedy, Defense Secretary Robert McNamara, Secretary of State Dean Rusk, Treasury Secretary Douglas Dillon, UN ambassador Adlai Stevenson, General Maxwell Taylor, McGeorge Bundy, Ted Sorensen, and Vice President Johnson were among those on the committee.

The members of the committee were sharply divided in their opinions about what should be done. Some wanted immediate bombing of the missile sites and invasion of Cuba. John and Robert Kennedy felt that this action would bring on an all-out nuclear war. Others thought that a naval blockade of Cuban shores might stop the construction of the missile sites. Bobby Kennedy and McNamara favored this approach, and that was the course of action the president decided to follow.

On Monday, October 22, President Kennedy spoke to the American people on television. He told them exactly what was happening. The whole nation was concerned.

The week dragged on, and messages flew back and forth between Khrushchev and Kennedy. Then eighteen Soviet cargo ships were spotted steaming toward Cuba, and Soviet submarines had been sent to protect them.

The president sent a message to Khrushchev demanding that the ships turn back, and that the missiles be removed from Cuba. Kennedy also demanded that the Soviet submarines turn back.

The cargo ships and their submarine escort drew closer. Finally, they stopped to await further orders. At the end of

IRBM LAUNCH SITE NO 1
GUANAJAY, CUBA
23 OCTOBER 1962

BATCH PLANTS

PRE-FAB CONSTRUCTION MATERIALS

NUCLEAR STORAGE BUNKER

LAUNCH PAD

CONTROL BUILDING

PROTECTED VEHICLE POSITIONS

LAUNCH PAD

This satellite photo details the missile site the Soviet Union was building in Cuba. When Kennedy learned of the site, he immediately set up a committee of trusted advisers to discuss what to do about it.

the week, the Soviet vessels turned and went back toward their homeland. Khrushchev had evidently given the order.

On Friday evening, October 26, the president received a message from Khrushchev that hinted at an agreement. The message was vague, but Khrushchev seemed to be saying that he would withdraw the missiles if the United States would promise not to invade Cuba. On Saturday Khrushchev sent another message that contradicted Friday's message. In the message, Khrushchev asked Kennedy to remove missiles from a base in Turkey in exchange for the Soviet Union removing its missiles from Cuba. The Soviet Union and Turkey shared a border at the time, and Khrushchev felt just as threatened by missiles there as Kennedy did by the missiles in Cuba.

Kennedy decided to act as though Khrushchev had offered a settlement and to ignore the Soviet leader's later statement. The president sent a letter in which he said the United States would accept the Soviet offer to remove the missiles from Cuba under UN supervision. In return, the United States promised not to invade Cuba and to halt the blockade. In secret, Kennedy also agreed to Khrushchev's demand to remove missiles from Turkey. Everyone waited tensely for the reply. The peace of the world hung in the balance.

Finally, a message came from the Soviet premier in a telegram: "The Soviet government has ordered the dismantling of bases and dispatching of equipment from the USSR [Soviet Union]. . . . I appreciate your assurance that the United States will not invade Cuba. Nikita Khrushchev."

CHAPTER NINE

REACHING FOR PEACE
AND FREEDOM

*"Genuine peace must be the product of many
nations, the sum of many acts. It must be
dynamic, not static, changing to meet the
challenge of each new generation."*

—John Kennedy, commencement address at
American University, Washington, D.C., June 10, 1963

When Kennedy became president, he decided that the United States should catch up with the Soviet Union in the field of space exploration. (The Soviets had launched a space capsule, *Sputnik I,* into orbit around Earth in 1957. In 1961 Soviet cosmonaut Yuri Gagarin became the first person to orbit Earth.) He said, "We have vowed that we shall see space filled not with weapons of mass destruction, but with instruments of knowledge and understanding." His goal was to land a person on the Moon by the end of the 1960s.

In 1962 John Glenn became the first American to orbit the Earth. Five years earlier, he had broken the transcontinental speed record, flying from California to New York in just 3 hours, 23 minutes, and 8.4 seconds.
✧ ———————————————

Scientists at the National Aeronautics and Space Administration (NASA) developed an Atlas rocket powerful enough to carry a man into space. In May 1961, Lieutenant Commander Alan Shepard became the first American to make a space flight. On February 20, 1962, John Glenn circled Earth three times. He was the first American to orbit Earth. Later, New York welcomed Glenn and President Kennedy with a ticker-tape parade.

The second U.S. piloted space flight took place on May 24, 1962, when Lieutenant Scott Carpenter orbited Earth three times in *Aurora 7*. Between October 4, 1961, and October 3, 1962, the United States placed forty-six satellites in orbit and launched four space probes to do basic research about space and piloted flight, to gather information about weather, communications, and navigation, and to photograph the surfaces of Venus and the Moon.

President Kennedy said, "The eyes of the world now look into space, to the Moon, and to the planets beyond, and we have vowed that we shall see space governed not by a hostile flag of conquest, but by a banner of freedom and peace." During this period, the Soviet Union and the United States were competing with each other in space development. Each country's leadership in science, engineering, and national defense was measured to a great degree by its success in space.

THE BERLIN WALL

Between the end of World War II in 1945 and the summer of 1961, about 3.5 million East Germans had left their homes and jobs to live in democratic West Berlin. Most East Germans fled to West Berlin (located within East Germany) because the Communist East German government had sealed off the border between East and West Germany. More than 30,000 East Germans had fled in July 1961 alone. They could not help noticing the freedom and relative wealth of West Berliners compared to their own way of life. The mass departure dramatized to the whole world the failure of the Communist system to meet the basic needs of its people. In August 1961, Khrushchev's response to this situation was to construct the Berlin Wall—a barrier of concrete and barbed wire guarded by soldiers and cutting through the heart of Berlin and dividing the city. The wall shocked the free world.

When President Kennedy visited West Germany in June 1963, he was appalled at his first sight of the wall—grim, gray, and forbidding. It kept apart German families, friends, and neighbors. Kennedy spoke to the huge crowd that filled the city square and streets in every direction. He told them:

> *Today, in the world of freedom, the proudest boast is "Ich bin ein Berliner." [I am a Berliner.] There are many people in the world today who really don't understand, or say they don't, what is the great issue between the free world and the*

A West German couple peers over the Berlin Wall. The wall caused much grief for the people of Berlin, as it separated many families who had been living in opposite sides of the city.

———————— ✧ ————————

Communist world. Let—them—come—to—Berlin! . . . All free men, wherever they may live, are citizens of Berlin, and therefore, as a free man, I take pride in the words, "Ich bin ein Berliner!"

"Ken-ne-dy! Ken-ne-dy!" the crowd chanted. There was no longer any doubt in the minds of the German people. They felt sure of the friendship of the United States.

A FAMILY VISIT

From Berlin Kennedy went to Dublin, Ireland, the home of his ancestors. The people treated him like a long-lost son. After Dublin, Kennedy traveled through the misty green countryside to Dunganstown in County Wexford.

This was where Kennedy's great-grandfather, Patrick Kennedy, had been born. President Kennedy's cousin, Mary Ryan, laid out a fine party in her yard. Every relative for miles around was an honored guest. After the party, Kennedy left for New Ross, Ireland.

Kennedy's great-grandfather had left New Ross to go to the United States. The people in New Ross presented Kennedy with a beautiful gold box. On the cover was the Kennedy coat of arms, and around the border was the Fitzgerald clan insignia.

Kennedy thanked them for the beautiful gift. His evident enjoyment and his ready Irish wit won their affection. Kennedy looked around at his relatives. "I'm glad to see," he remarked, "some of the Kennedys missed the boat and didn't all go to Washington." Kennedy returned from his successful

✧

Kennedy poses with his cousins and other family members during his trip to Ireland in 1963.

tour with the admiration and trust of the German people and with the hearts of the Irish in his keeping.

CRAFTING A TREATY

One of the first things Kennedy wanted to do when he returned to Washington was to finalize the negotiations for the nuclear test ban treaty with the Soviet Union. He had laid the groundwork for the treaty when he met with Khrushchev in Austria in 1961. Kennedy bent all his efforts toward achieving his goal.

Finally, after months of quiet talks with the Soviets, Kennedy's efforts began to bear fruit. Earlier in 1963, Kennedy had postponed nuclear tests in Nevada to show that the United States was serious about a test ban treaty. The Soviets also indicated that they might be interested in banning nuclear tests.

Many meetings took place to work out the terms of the treaty. By July Great Britain, the Soviet Union, and the United States had agreed on the main points related to banning nuclear tests in the earth's atmosphere. On July 25, representatives from the three nations initialed copies of the treaty in Moscow. Kennedy appeared on television and told the American people:

> *I speak to you tonight in a spirit of hope. . . . [Since] the advent of nuclear weapons, all mankind has been struggling to escape from the darkening prospect of mass destruction on earth. . . . Yesterday a shaft of light cut into the darkness. . . . This treaty is not the millennium. . . . But it is an important first step—a step*

toward peace, a step toward reason, a step away
from war. . . . According to the ancient Chinese
proverb, "A journey of 1000 miles must begin with
a single step. . . . " Let us take that first step.

On September 24, 1963, the U.S. Senate ratified the
Nuclear Test Ban Treaty, and it became effective for all three
countries on October 10. As he signed the treaty, Kennedy
said, "The age of nuclear energy has been full of fear, yet
never empty of hope. Today the fear is a little less and the
hope is a little greater. . . . I hereby pledge, on behalf of the
United States, if this treaty fails it will not be our doing."

The Nuclear Test Ban Treaty may have been John
Kennedy's crowning achievement. But he still had many
serious problems. One of the most serious was the conflict
in Vietnam, in Southeast Asia.

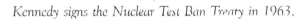

Kennedy signs the Nuclear Test Ban Treaty in 1963.

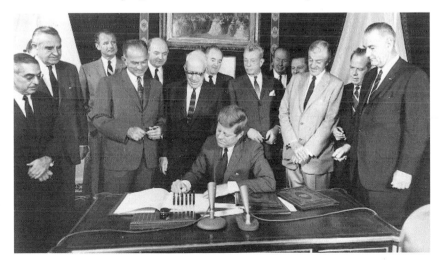

Supporters of Ho Chi Minh (left) wanted to unite North and South Vietnam under his Communist leadership. Many South Vietnamese thought Ngo Dinh Diem (right) was a cruel leader, and they were eager for a new ruler.

———————————————— ✧ ————————————————

THE WAR IN VIETNAM

In 1954 an international conference had divided Vietnam into North Vietnam and South Vietnam. The purpose of the conference was to arrange a peace settlement after France was defeated in its attempt to maintain colonial rule of Vietnam. The settlement also called for an election in 1956 to unite Vietnam under one government.

North Vietnam was under Communist control. Its leader, Premier Ho Chi Minh, had led a revolutionary group, called the Vietminh, in the fight for independence from French rule. Ho Chi Minh was strongly allied with Communist China.

In 1955 Ngo Dinh Diem had been chosen as the leader of South Vietnam. Diem's government was harsh, though anti-Communist. Claiming that the Communist Party would not permit fair elections, Diem refused to allow the 1956 election to take place. His continued oppression and indifference to the needs of his people caused a virtual civil war. One group of Vietnamese people supported President Diem. Another group, members of the Vietminh, later called Viet Cong, supported Ho Chi Minh. The latter group wanted all of Vietnam united under Ho Chi Minh's leadership. The Viet Cong were trained in guerrilla warfare by Communist North Vietnam, which was aided by Communist China. Guerrilla warfare consists of striking quick blows from an ambush and then disappearing into the trackless jungle or countryside.

While Eisenhower was still president, South Vietnam had asked the United States for help in fighting the guerrilla raids by the Viet Cong. It was difficult for soldiers trained in conventional methods of warfare, as Diem's army was, to fight against these kinds of attacks.

President Eisenhower had sent supplies and military advisers to help train the South Vietnamese army. Kennedy was left with this commitment when he became president. Late in 1961, he sent more advisers, helicopters, and supplies.

Although the United States kept sending more people and more supplies every year, the Viet Cong showed no signs of backing down. At the same time, the war itself was creating a serious division among people in the United States. Many viewed it as a civil war that had to be decided by the Vietnamese people themselves—without another country interfering.

Kennedy told his brother Bobby that, after the upcoming election in 1964, his first priority would be to get the

United States out of Vietnam. He had come to believe that the war in Vietnam was a political struggle within that country and that the United States had no reason to be there.

LOOKING AHEAD

In August 1963, Jacqueline gave birth to a baby son, Patrick. Patrick died shortly after birth of a breathing difficulty. Both Kennedy and his wife were grief-stricken. Caroline and John had been promised a baby brother, and they were disappointed.

Still, the president's busy schedule went on, filled with meetings, speeches, and press conferences. Kennedy was good at ad-libbing, although he was usually well informed about most issues and could anticipate reporters' questions. When he was asked an unexpected question, his witty answers usually got him out of difficulties and delighted his audience.

The upcoming election in 1964 was on Kennedy's mind. As it drew nearer, he looked to Vice President Johnson for help in Johnson's home state of Texas. The Democrats in Texas were bitterly divided into two camps: supporters of conservative Governor John Connally and supporters of the more liberal Senator Ralph Yarborough. Texas was too important a state to lose. If the Democrats were fighting among themselves, it might be easy for a Republican candidate to win. Kennedy thought visiting Texas with Vice President Johnson might help to heal the breach.

CHAPTER TEN

A TRAGIC END

*"If we all can persevere, if we can in every
land and office look beyond our own shores
and ambitions, then surely the age will dawn
in which the strong are just and the weak
secure and the peace preserved."*
—John F. Kennedy, in an address to the United
Nations, September 25, 1961

John Kennedy knew that a segment of the population in
Texas, a southern state, did not approve of his stand on civil
rights. But he was sure that differences of opinion could be
solved through reason and goodwill. He was, in fact, plan-
ning to talk about reason and goodwill in his speech at a
lunch at the Dallas Texas Trade Mart in November 1963.
During the flight to Dallas, Kennedy put finishing touches
on the speech. The concluding paragraph read:

We . . . in this generation are—by destiny rather

*than by choice—the watchmen on the walls of
freedom. We ask therefore . . . that we may exer-
cise our strength with wisdom and restraint—and
that we may achieve in our time and for all time
the ancient vision of "peace on earth, goodwill
toward men." That must always be our goal. . . .*

Jacqueline accompanied her husband to Texas. Their first
stop on November 21 was in San Antonio, where many of
the people were of Mexican descent. Kennedy had been
invited to dedicate a new aerospace medical center there.
The way from the airport to the center was lined with
cheering, enthusiastic people. They threw handfuls of colorful confetti and carried hand-lettered signs saying
"*Bienvenido* [welcome] Mr. President and Jackie." Jacqueline
enjoyed the welcome as much as Jack, and she spoke to the
delighted people in perfect Spanish.

The presidential party flew from San Antonio to Houston
and then on to Fort Worth, where they were to spend the
night. Although there were scattered signs in both cities saying
things like, "Ban the Brothers" and "Kennedy, Khrushchev,
and King," and editorials in the newspapers calling the president a traitor, crowds were friendly for the most part.

On the morning of November 22, Kennedy met in the
hotel parking lot with some of the "ordinary" people of Fort
Worth—mechanics, truck drivers, secretaries, clerks, house-
wives—who, Kennedy said, were his true constituents (voters
who elect a person to represent them). Later he and Jacqueline
were to be the luncheon guests of the Fort Worth Chamber of
Commerce. When Jacqueline appeared in the hotel dining
room, looking beautiful in a pink suit and a matching hat,

there was an audible stir of admiration. Reporters gathered around her. The president, delighted, quipped, "Why is it no one cares what Lyndon and I wear?"

It was a short plane hop from Fort Worth to Dallas. When their plane landed at Love Field, the president and Jacqueline received an ovation. People kept pushing their hands through the airport fence to try to touch the president or shake his hand. The mayor's wife presented Jacqueline with a bouquet of red roses.

Because they were concerned about the president's safety, the Secret Service had shipped a bubble-top car to Dallas for the

President and Mrs. Kennedy arrive in Dallas.
———— ✧ ————

president's use. The top was a removable, see-through cover that allowed spectators and occupants to see, while at the same time protecting the riders from weather or the press of the crowds. It had rained earlier, but the weather had turned warm and sunny. Jack insisted that the bubble top be removed. So far, the welcome had been warm and sincere, and there had been no threatening or hostile incidents. Fears for the president's safety had faded away.

THE DALLAS MOTORCADE

About 250,000 people lined the streets in Dallas along the route of the presidential motorcade. As the cars approached

Dealey Plaza—a wide, grass-covered area—three streets came together: Houston, Elm, and Main. The presidential car made a sharp turn north onto Elm. The Texas School Book Depository, a dull orange brick building, was on the right. The road dipped downhill at that point.

A Secret Service agent drove the car, and another agent sat next to him with a rifle close at hand. Governor and Mrs. Connally sat in front of Jacqueline and the president, who occupied the back seat. Secret Service agents also rode in a car following the presidential party.

Mrs. Connally turned around and said to the president, "You can't say Dallas wasn't friendly." At that moment, a sharp, cracking sound, like an auto backfiring, pierced the air. Jacqueline, who had been waving to the people on her left, turned to face Kennedy. His hand went to his throat, and he began to fall forward. At almost the same time, the governor gave a sharp cry and bent over. Both President Kennedy and John Connally had been shot. Seconds later there was another shot, and the back of the president's head was torn away.

Jacqueline saw Clint Hill, a Secret Service agent, trying to climb from the street onto the back of the car. She crawled toward Hill and held out her hand to him. He scrambled in and pushed Jacqueline down. He threw himself over the president's body to shield him.

The presidential car drew out of line and raced to the nearest hospital while agents radioed ahead. Doctors and orderlies met the president's car at the entrance to Parkland Memorial Hospital. They rushed the body of the president to Trauma Room One. Governor Connally was taken to another emergency room.

Everything possible was done to save the president, but it was hopeless. He had no pulse, no blood pressure. John Connally's wound was serious, but not fatal.

Vice President Johnson, not knowing if the shooting was part of a conspiracy or the act of one person, decided he should get back to Washington at once. In a short time, the president's body was carried onto *Air Force One.* Jacqueline, Vice President Johnson, Mrs. Johnson, and other members of the presidential party boarded the plane for Washington.

Inside the plane, Lyndon Johnson took the oath of office, administered by Judge Sarah Hughes. Lyndon Johnson became the thirty-sixth president of the United States. Jacqueline

——————————————— ✧ ———————————————

A solemn Lyndon B. Johnson takes the oath of office aboard
Air Force One *shortly after Kennedy's assassination.*

Kennedy stood, dazed and numb with shock, unmindful of her bloodstained clothes, beside the new president.

A FINAL FAREWELL

The day after its return from Dallas, President Kennedy's body lay in its flag-draped casket, on the same bier, or stand, that had held the body of Abraham Lincoln in the Rotunda of the Capitol. All day and all evening, people filed past the casket. Lines of people, six abreast, stood in bitter cold for hours, waiting for a chance to say good-bye to their president.

After the doors of the Rotunda were closed to the public, Jacqueline and Caroline paid one last visit while mourning officials looked on. They knelt before the closed casket and said some prayers. Caroline reached up and touched the flag draping the casket, as though the act could bring her father closer.

John Kennedy's funeral was attended by kings, princesses and princes, presidents, prime ministers, and representatives of ninety-two countries from

——————— ✧

In a final farewell, Caroline reaches up to touch her father's casket.

around the world, and by millions of grieving U.S. citizens. Many lined the streets of Washington. Others watched on television.

A simple Mass for the Dead was held at the Cathedral of St. Matthew in Washington, D.C. Jacqueline held the hands of John Jr. and Caroline as they came out of the church and stood on the steps. A riderless black horse, a sword dangling at its side and stirrups hanging backward from the saddle, trotted beside the caisson (a two-wheeled cart) with the body of the fallen leader in its casket. Six gray horses pulled the caisson. It was November 25, 1963, John Jr.'s third birthday. The little boy gravely put his hand to his head and saluted the casket of his dead father.

Jacqueline Kennedy walked the mile or so from the cathedral to Arlington Cemetery, Robert Kennedy beside her. Many of those attending the Mass followed her. Cardinal Cushing gave the last blessing for the dead. Just as the cardinal finished his prayer, fifty jet fighter planes zoomed overhead. Troops on the ground presented arms. A twenty-one-gun salute sounded. The strains of taps sounded over the grave. The flag that covered the casket was removed, folded, and placed in Jacqueline's hands. For a moment, Jacqueline's self-control threatened to break, but she regained her composure and stepped into the waiting limousine.

THE KENNEDY PRESIDENCY

The sound of laughter was very much a part of the spirit of John Kennedy. There was a gaiety about him, a joy and zest for living that no amount of pain could subdue. The ability to laugh at himself was no small part of his charm. He took the world and its problems seriously—never himself.

A sense of urgency ran through all of his actions, as though the tasks he had set for himself could only be accomplished by ceaseless effort, and time was short. He was the first president to be born in the twentieth century, and he was very much a man of his time. He was restless, seeking, with a thirst for knowledge, and he had a feeling of deep commitment, not only to the people of the United States, but to the peoples of the world.

To balance his idealism, he had the advantage of a logical mind. He had the ability to look at problems clearly and to focus the full power of his mind on their solutions.

Some critics have said that John Kennedy's presidency lacked "greatness." Still, many of the things he fought for—the rights of minorities, the poor, the very old and the very young, aid to education, better understanding among the peoples of the world—have come closer to being realized because of John Kennedy. It was he who set things in motion, he who moved the world in the direction of peace and cooperation. There was nothing small about John Kennedy. His dreams and hopes were big. His courage was monumental. His shadow still lies long across the land.

EPILOGUE

Soon after the assassination, the Texas School Book Depository was swarming with police and Secret Service agents. A fifteen-year-old boy had told a policeman that he'd seen something sticking out of a sixth-floor window as the presidential motorcade passed by. After a roll call of depository employees, only one person was missing—Lee Harvey Oswald, a shipping clerk.

Later on the afternoon of November 22, 1963, Oswald was arrested for the murder of John Kennedy. But Oswald never had his day in court. Two days later, as he was being transferred from a cell in the Dallas jail to a maximum security cell in the county jail, Jack Ruby, a Dallas dance-hall owner, shot Oswald. He died around 1:00 P.M.

Jack Ruby was arrested and stood trial in Dallas. He was found guilty and was sentenced to hang. He died in jail, of cancer, on January 3, 1967.

TIMELINE

1917 John Fitzgerald Kennedy is born on May 29 in Brookline, Massachusetts, to Joseph P. Kennedy and Rose Fitzgerald Kennedy.

1934 Kennedy graduates from Choate Preparatory.

1940 Kennedy graduates cum laude from Harvard University. *Why England Slept*, Kennedy's first book, is published.

1941 Kennedy joins the U.S. Navy. On December 7, Japan bombs Pearl Harbor, Hawaii, bringing the United States into World War II.

1943 In August Kennedy makes a heroic rescue of his crew after a Japanese destroyer rams and sinks their boat.

1944 In June Kennedy receives the Purple Heart and a Navy and Marine Corps Medal. Joseph P. Kennedy Jr. is killed during a flying mission in Europe. President Franklin Delano Roosevelt is elected to a fourth term.

1946 Kennedy is elected to Congress.

1952 Kennedy is elected to the U.S. Senate.

1953 Kennedy marries Jacqueline Bouvier on September 12 at Saint Mary's Church in Newport, Rhode Island.

1954 Kennedy undergoes back surgery and almost dies. On May 17, in *Brown v. Board of Education of Topeka,* the Supreme Court ruled that segregation in public schools is unconstitutional.

1955 Kennedy undergoes a second back surgery—this time successfully.

1956 Kennedy's second book, *Profiles in Courage,* is published and wins the Pulitzer Prize. At the Democratic National

Convention in Chicago, Kennedy makes the nominating speech for presidential candidate Adlai Stevenson

1957   Daughter Caroline Kennedy is born on November 27.

1958   Kennedy is reelected to the Senate.

1960   Kennedy wins the presidential nomination at the Democratic National Convention in Los Angeles. On November 8, he is elected president of the United States. John F. Kennedy Jr. is born on November 25.

1961   Kennedy is inaugurated on January 20. He establishes the Peace Corps. He becomes involved in the ongoing civil rights movement. In March he initiates the Alliance for Progress. The unsuccessful Bay of Pigs invasion occurs on April 17. In June he meets separately with President Charles de Gaulle of France, Prime Minister Harold Macmillan of Great Britain, and Premier Nikita Khrushchev of the Soviet Union. In December he travels to Venezuela and Colombia.

1962   On February 20, astronaut John Glenn circles Earth. On May 24, Lieutenant Scott Carpenter orbits Earth in *Aurora 7*. In October Kennedy successfully confronts the Cuban Missile Crisis. Brother Ted Kennedy is elected to the U.S. Senate.

1963   Kennedy visits West Berlin and his relatives in Ireland. He sends his civil rights bill to Congress on June 19. The March on Washington takes place on August 28. He negotiates the Nuclear Test Ban Treaty with the Soviet Union and Great Britain. Congress approves it on September 24. Son Patrick is born in August but dies shortly after birth. On November 22, Kennedy is assassinated in Dallas, Texas. His body is buried on November 25, John Jr.'s third birthday.

SOURCE NOTES

7 Luke 12:48 (New Oxford Annotated Bible).

9 Charles Kenney, *John F. Kennedy* (New York: Perseus Books Group, 2000), 5.

15 John F. Kennedy, *Profiles in Courage* (New York: Harper and Row, 1956), 215–216.

17 Nigel Hamilton, *JFK: Reckless Youth* (New York: Random House, 1992), 243.

21 John F. Kennedy, letter to his parents, received September 23, 1943. Quoted in Herbert S. Parmet, *Jack: The Struggles of John F. Kennedy* (New York: The Dial Press, 1980), 107.

23 Geoffrey Perret, *Jack: A Life Like No Other* (New York: Random House, 2001), 111.

23 Ibid.

23 Ibid.

26 Hamilton, 591.

29 "Lt. John F. Kennedy's NMCM Citation," *Department of the Navy Naval Historical Center,* 1997, <http://www.history.navy.mil/faqs/faq60-10.htm> (November 14, 2003).

30 Kennedy, *Profiles,* 216.

31 Parmet, 132.

43 Theodore C. Sorensen, *Kennedy* (New York: Harper and Row, 1965), 153.

47 Peter Collier and David Horowitz, *The Kennedys: An American Drama* (New York: Summit Books, 1984), 237–238.

48 Ibid.

52 Jacques Lowe, *Portrait: The Emergence of John F. Kennedy* (New York: Bramhall House, 1961), 129.

54 Sorensen, 165.

54 John F. Kennedy, "Address of Senator John F. Kennedy Accepting the Democratic Nomination for the Presidency of the United States, July 15, 1960," *John F.*

Kennedy Library and Museum, 2002, <http://www.jfklibrary.org/j071560.htm> (August 4, 2003).

55 John F. Kennedy, "Inaugural Address, January 20, 1961," *John F. Kennedy Library and Museum,* 2002, <http://www.jfklibrary.org/j012061.htm> (November 17, 2003).

56–57 John F. Kennedy, "Speech of Senator John F. Kennedy, Boston Garden, Boston, MA, November 7, 1960," *JFK Link,* 1999, <http://www.jfklink.com/speeches/jfk/nov60/jfk071160_boston02.html> (August 5, 2003).

57 "Flashback 1960: Kennedy Beats Nixon," *BBC News,* 2000, <http:news.bbc.co.uk/1/hi/world/americas/1015074.stm>. (December 17, 2003)

58 Lowe, 168.

58 Ibid.

58 Perret, 272.

60 Collier and Horowitz, 256.

63 Robert Frost, "The Gift Outright," *Robert Frost.org,* 1999, <http://www.robertfrost.org/jfk.html> (August 5, 2003).

63–64 John F. Kennedy, "Inaugural Address, January 20, 1961," *John F. Kennedy Library and Museum,* 2002, <http://www.jfklibrary.org/j012061.htm> (August 5, 2003).

65 John F. Kennedy, "Address of Senator John F. Kennedy Accepting the Democratic Nomination for the Presidency of the United States, July 15, 1960," *John F. Kennedy Library and Museum,* 2002, <http://www.jfklibrary.org/j071560.htm> (August 4, 2003).

66 "New Exhibit to Profile Kennedy Dinner for Nobel Laureates," February 11, 1999, *John F. Kennedy Library and Museum,* 1999, <http://www.jfklibrary.org/pr_nobel_lauriates.html> (August 5, 2003).

70 "Renewing the Call to Public Service," *Common Dreams News Center,* 2001, <http://www.commondreams.org/views01/0310-02.htm> (December 17, 2003).

70–71 John F. Kennedy, "Radio and Television Report to the American People on Civil Rights," *John F. Kennedy Library and Museum,* 2002, <http://www.jfklibrary.org/j061163.htm> (August 5, 2003).

73 John F. Kennedy, "Radio and Television Report to the Nation on the Situation at the University of Mississippi," *John F. Kennedy Library and Museum,* 2002, <http://www.jfklibrary.org/j093062.htm> (August 5, 2003).

74 John F. Kennedy, "Radio and Television Report to the American People on Civil Rights," *John F. Kennedy Library and Museum,* 2002, <http://www.jfklibrary.org/j061163.htm> (August 5, 2003).

74 Ibid.

74 "Farewell America," *JFK Online,* June 11, 1963, <http://www.jfk-online.com/farewell12.html> (August 5, 2003).

74 Martin Luther King Jr., "I Have a Dream," *Holidays on the Net,* 2003, <http://www.holidays.net.mlk/speech.htm> (August 5, 2003).

76 John F. Kennedy, "Inaugural Address, January 20, 1961," *John F. Kennedy Library and Museum,* 2002, <http://www.jfklibrary.org/j012061.htm> (August 5, 2003).

78 Sorensen, 308.

79 Ibid., 537.

84 "The Cold War: A CNN Perspectives Series," *CNN Interactive,* 1999, <http://www.cnn.com/SPECIALS/cold.war/episodes/10/script.html> (August 5, 2003).

85 John F. Kennedy, "Commencement Address at American University, June 10, 1963," *John F. Kennedy Library and Museum,* 2002, <http://www.jfklibrary.org/j061063.htm> (December 17, 2003).

85 John F. Kennedy, "Address at Rice University on the Nation's Space Effort," *John F. Kennedy Library and Museum,* 2002, <http://www.jfklibrary.org/lesson_space_race.html> (August 5, 2003).

86 Ibid.

87–88 John F. Kennedy, "Remarks in the Rudolph Wilde Platz," *John F. Kennedy Library and Museum,* June 26, 1963, <http://www.jfklibrary.org/j062663.htm> (August 5, 2003).

89 Sorensen, 582.

90–91 John F. Kennedy, "Radio and Tele-vision Address to the American People on the Nuclear Test Ban Treaty," *John F. Kennedy Library and Museum,* 2002, <http://www.jfklibrary.org/jfk_test_ban_speech.html> (August 5, 2003).

91 Max Cleland, "Remarks by Senator Max Cleland on the Comprehensive Test Ban Treaty," *Council for a Livable World,* October 13, 1999, <http://www.clw.org/pub/clw/coalition/cleland101399.htm> (August 5, 2003).

95 John F. Kennedy, "Address to the United Nations, September 25, 1961," *John F. Kennedy Library and Museum,* 2002, <http://www.jfklibrary.org/j092561.htm> (December 17, 2003).

95–96 John F. Kennedy, "Remarks Prepared for Delivery at the Trade Mart in Dallas, Texas, November 22, 1963," *John F. Kennedy Library and Museum,* 2002, <http://www.jfklibrary.org/j112263b.htm> (August 5, 2003).

97 "The Hours Before Dallas: A Recollection by President Kennedy's Fort Worth Advance Man," *U.S. National Archives and Records Administration,* 2000, <http://www.archives.gov/publications/prologue/summer_2000_jfk_last_day_3.html> (August 5, 2003).

98 Perret, 398.

SELECTED BIBLIOGRAPHY

Burns, James MacGregor. *John Kennedy, A Political Profile*. New York: Harcourt Brace and Co., 1959.

Collier, Peter, and David Horowitz. *The Kennedys: An American Drama*. New York: Summit Books, 1984.

Donovan, Robert J. *PT 109*. New York: McGraw Hill, 1961.

Johnson, Haynes. *The Bay of Pigs*. New York: W. W. Norton, 1964.

Kennedy, John F. *Profiles in Courage*. New York: Harper and Row, 1956.

Kennedy, Robert F. *Thirteen Days*. New York: New American Library, Inc. 1969.

Lincoln, Evelyn. *My Twelve Years with John F. Kennedy*. New York: David McKay, 1965.

Lowe, Jacques. *Portrait: The Emergence of John F. Kennedy*. New York: Bramhall House, 1961.

Luce, Iris, ed. *Letters from the Peace Corps*. Washington, D.C.: Robert B. Luce, Inc., 1964.

Manchester, William. *Portrait of a President*. Boston: Little, Brown, 1962.

Martin, Ralph G. *A Hero for Our Times*. New York: MacMillan, 1980.

Schlesinger, Jr., Arthur M. *A Thousand Days*. New York: Houghton Mifflin, 1965.

Seaborg, Glenn T. *Kennedy, Khrushchev, and the Test Ban Treaty*. Los Angeles: University of California Press, 1981.

Sorensen, Theodore C. *Kennedy*. New York: Harper and Row, 1965.

FURTHER READING AND WEBSITES

Biography of John F. Kennedy <http://www.whitehouse.gov/history/presidents/jk35.html> The official White House site offers a short biography of the nation's thirty-fifth president.

Darby, Jean. *Dwight D. Eisenhower*. Minneapolis: Lerner Publications Company, 2004

Falkof, Lucille. *John F. Kennedy*. Ada, OK: Garrett Educational Corporation, 1988.

John Fitzgerald Kennedy: A Life in Pictures. New York: Phaidon Press, 2003.

John Fitzgerald Kennedy Library <http://www.cs.umb.edu/jfklibrary/>. This website offers extensive information about the life of John F. Kennedy, including biographies, photos, films, speeches, and more.

John F. Kennedy National Historic Site <http://www.nps.gov/jofi/>. This website is a travel guide to the birthplace and childhood home of John F. Kennedy.

Kennedy, John F. *Why England Slept*. New York: Harper and Row, 1956.

Lazo, Caroline Evensen. *Harry S. Truman*. Minneapolis: Lerner Publications Company, 2003.

Levy, Debbie. *Lyndon B. Johnson*. Minneapolis: Lerner Publications Company, 2003.

———. *The Vietnam War*. Minneapolis: Lerner Publications Company, 2004.

Manheimer, Ann S. *Martin Luther King Jr*. Minneapolis: Carolrhoda Books, Inc., 2005.

Márquez, Herón. *Richard M. Nixon*. Minneapolis: Lerner Publications Company, 2003.

Randall, Marta. *John F. Kennedy*. New York: Chelsea House, 1988.

Roberts, Jeremy. *Franklin D. Roosevelt*. Minneapolis: Lerner Publications Company, 2003.

Schwarz, Urs. *John F. Kennedy*. London: Paul Hamlyn, 1964.

Selfridge, John W. *John F. Kennedy: Courage in Crisis*. New York: Fawcett Columbine, 1989.

White, Theodore H. *The Making of the President 1960*. New York: Atheneum, 1961.

Williams, Barbara. *World War II—The Pacific*. Minneapolis: Lerner Publications Company, 2005.

INDEX

ABOUT THE AUTHOR

Catherine Corley Anderson graduated with honors from the School of the Art Institute of Chicago. She did graduate work in psychology and education at St. Xavier College, Northwestern University, and the University of Chicago. During that whole period, Ms. Anderson was also writing. She has had many stories, articles, and poems published in children's magazines. *John F. Kennedy* is among her several published books.

PHOTO ACKNOWLEDGMENTS

The images in this book are used with the permission of: The White House, pp. 1, 7, 15, 21, 30, 43, 55, 65, 76, 85, 95, 103; The John F. Kennedy Library, pp. 2 [ST-C237-1-63], 6 [KN-C19364], 9 [PC 8], 18 [FYT22], 22 [PC100], 29 [FF 298], 34 [PC 365], 37 [PX 65-25:21], 38 [PC 473], 41 [PC 780], 45, 59 [AR6287-E], 66 [KN-21219], 69 [AR 7405 D], 83 [PX66-20:19], 89 [ST-C232-4-63], 97 [STC420-13-63], 99, 100 [AR 8255-12]; © CORBIS, pp. 10, 46; Franklin D. Roosevelt Library, p. 13; © Hulton/Archive by Getty Images, pp. 14, 80 (all); © Hulton-Deutsch Collection/CORBIS, pp. 16, 75; Laura Westlund, p. 27; National Archives, pp. 31, 32, 51, 56, 92 (right); *The New Bedford Standard-Times,* p. 39; U.S. Army, p. 40; Marty Nordstrom Photo, Minnesota Historical Society, p. 50; © Bettmann/CORBIS, pp. 53, 62, 73, 88; The Everett Collection, p. 54; Office of the Senator, p. 60; © Bettmann; Stanley Tretick, 1963/CORBIS, p. 67; Photo by *The Birmingham News,* 2003, p. 72; Historical Association of Southern Florida, p. 78; Courtesy of the U.S. Air Force Museum, p. 86; Defense Nuclear Agency, p. 91; Library of Congress, p. 92 (left) [LC-USZ62-126586]

Front cover: Minnesota State Democratic Farmer Labor Committee.